CW01512365

Ancient Britain

For Modern Folk

Tom Howells

Revellers celebrate the Summer Solstice at Stonehenge (p. 32).

Contents

Timeline of Ancient Britain

The period referred to as prehistoric or 'ancient' covers close to a million years. In anthropological terms, it's broken into three ages: the Stone Age, Bronze Age and Iron Age. The Stone Age – when humans lived as hunter-gatherers – saw the first evidence of human occupation in what we now know as the British Isles, although we have scant evidence of what life was like. Our timeline begins in the final aeons of this era, when humans first began to form settled societies.

Neolithic (late Stone Age)

These millennia saw a shift from hunter-gatherer to more complex agricultural societies, with people building permanent settlements, clearing forests for farming and domesticating animals. Construction on some of the more grandiose monuments, like Stonehenge (p.32) and Avebury (p.50), began around 3000 BCE. Many burial chambers survive from this period, including earth mounds, stone dolmens and quoits, plus some early stone circles.

Bronze Age	Iron Age	Roman Britain
2500 BCE – 800 BCE	800 BCE – 43 CE	

Bronze Age

As the name suggests, an era defined by the emergence of early metalwork. Societies became more hierarchical, and barrows, cairns and cist graves designed to house just one occupant rather than many reflect this. Farming intensified, leading to larger settlements. Communities expanded and spread across Britain, constructing stone monuments in new places.

Iron Age

A period demarcated by a wider embrace of iron tools and weapons. Increased tribal warfare meant more hillforts, eminently recognisable for their grassy ramparts and earth-works. Trade links with Europe increased, culminating in the Roman invasion of 43 CE – ending Britain's Iron Age.

Introduction

I don't recall exactly when I began communing with the ancients. But *where* is simple enough. The Isle of Wight's tumbledown folds are dotted with esoteric points of interest: in particular, a host of mounds rising from the precipitous downland and dense woodland, and the Longstone (p.88), a towering rock perched dramatically above the Channel (and a home-from-home for local Pagans, who still decorate its lichen-y surfaces with seasonal offerings).

Both seemed innocuous at first – the mounds more than the whacking megalith, admittedly. But as their bygone significance (and status as burial sites) became clear through return visits embellished by my own casual reading, they were suffused with a kind of mystical, timeslip energy. Cyclically ambling back, week on week, year on year, I was rapt.

The three decades since have seen my own steady (if hobbyist) immersion in other ancient zones around the country, and especially the monumental gems of Southwest England. And I'm not alone. It seems a generation of stone 'heads' has been simultaneously embracing Britain's ancient nuclei, drawn by the same escapist impulses that I have been. There's no doubt that our collective interest in these recondite places has grown again; their appeal transcends the academic for something more holistically existential.

In a hyper-connected age of relentless mental fatigue, all the world's information literally at our fingertips, perhaps it's the allure of an accessible, ubiquitous connection to an unknowable past. Perhaps it's the hazy melding of natural beauty and deep history? The imposing stature of the rocks themselves? Or just a fresh flex for our Hinge profiles? Maybe it's something of all of them.

Who were the ancient Britons?

'Ancient Britain' was a sprawling period of thousands of years, covering the Neolithic era, Bronze Age and Iron Age (to say nothing of the blurry aeons before and after). Over this time, humans transitioned from being hunter-gatherers to farmers, settling the land, forming communities and constructing the monuments we see in this book – all without the written records that might give us an idea of the mindsets and socio-cultural contexts that drove them. Attempting to get a handle on just *who* created these eye-catching places is a reasonable endeavour, albeit one hindered by the mists of time.

First, they weren't all technically 'Britons': the agrarian cultures of Neolithic Britain shared ancestry with people who had travelled from northwest Anatolia (what is now Turkey), while the Bronze Age saw great waves of migration from Europe that effectively replaced the Neolithic population en masse.

Neither were they people with a consistent set of beliefs and spiritual practices – but there is some clear regularity in the profound regard for death and the afterlife in many of the monuments they created. There's a pervading idea that prehistoric Britain was a bit of an underdeveloped backwater compared to mainland Europe and its civilisations, but it's undeniable that building such monuments required sheer chutzpah and eye-popping ambition – as some of what follows will reveal.

Why are these sites here?

This question has haunted antiquarians for centuries, and the answer is frustratingly vague. Detailed excavations and more modern methods of radiocarbon dating have given fair estimates as to the age of these places, but their practical purposes remain rather foggy. Many are tombs, often with alignments to the sunrises at the solstices; that much is known. Some of the others are more abstruse. Over time, archaeologists and historians have posited various theories as to their uses, from ceremonial funerary sites to recherché gathering places, regal graves, lunar temples, sweat lodges and sacred celestial clocks. The only thing we can say with absolute certainty is that we are uncertain.

Why do we know so little about them?

In short, because there is no writing. The scant literacy of these ancient civilisations (minimal in the Bronze Age and non-existent in the Neolithic) means there simply aren't any records explaining why these things were built. Archaeological finds from these eras give some insight into the practicalities of peoples' lives, but the existential reasons for the construction of the more overtly mysterious ritual sites remain unclear. So, it's back to wondering.

For centuries upon centuries, people seemed to give far less of a hoot about these bewildering locations than we do now. Properly documented excavations didn't begin until the mid-1600s, when pioneering archaeologists like John Aubrey recorded monuments in southern England for the first time (see p.202 for more). The exploration of tombs really took off in the Victorian era, when antiquarian treasure hunting was the fashion of the age.

What's more, it's supposed that many of the missing stones in incomplete circles and complexes were probably taken as building materials for walls, houses and bridges over the millennia – a brazen impulse that seems insane to modern minds. Perhaps if more of these places had been left respectfully complete, there'd be a tad more information to glean.

Why should we visit them now?

Mulling the bigger picture question of 'why now?' is where the 'ancient' and 'modern' of our title collide. For one, Paganism is seeing a renaissance in Britain, with 74,000 people identifying as such in a 2022 census. Its customs embrace a connection with nature and a more elemental, seasonal life, and the places in this book are a brilliant conduit for reconnecting with the land around us. (Quite whether the readers of cool stone-related zines like *Weird Walk* are true followers of polytheism is another question, but both trends speak to a growing appetite for living in tune with the land.)

The places in this book have long been arenas for spiritual and countercultural gathering – most clearly seen

9

in the 1990s 'free parties' at Stonehenge, and the pilgrimage of New Age, druidic and hippie groups to Salisbury Plain each Summer Solstice. As COVID-19 has readjusted our priorities in life, some of these once-alternative concerns and ideas – of peace and a more immediate participation with the world around us – have drifted mainstream. These sites represent fascinating hubs for a new (or rather, very, very old) kind of community engagement that transcends the partisan, politicised stresses of everyday life, offering a remedy to modern burnout. With the world's predilection for Big Tech, free-market neoliberalism and rank political populism, perhaps it's nice to simply retreat somewhere quiet and ageless, to forget the quagmire that is Earth 2025.

It's crucial to add that this book provides just a snapshot of the ancient landscape. Thousands of these monuments exist across what's now known as Great Britain in various states of size and repair. But with any luck, from the most elaborate complex to each lonely monolith, this book will provide a little insight into a bevy of magical places offering a tangible connection to an arcane world – and the people that populated it – that remains tantalisingly out of reach.

Tom Howells
London, 2025

Ancient Architecture

There's a whole dictionary of specific terms used to describe ancient monuments – many of which can appear rather confusing, old-fashioned or outright academic. Here are some key words that pop up throughout this book.

Megalith

Simply, a large stone forming part of an ancient monument, whether standing up or not. 'Megalithic' describes any ancient monument containing huge stones.

Menhir

A large stone that is stood up one end and forms part of a group of similar stones. Menhirs are sometimes called 'uprights'.

Monolith

Any large stone that stands alone.

Recumbent

Any large stone that lies on its side, appearing a bit like an altar – see below.

Trilithon

An ancient structure comprising two upright stones and one laid across the top, like the kinds at Stonehenge.

Capstone

A flat slab of a rock used as the 'roof' part of a **chamber**.

Barrow

An ancient burial **mound**, often containing a **chamber**. They can be round or elongated, like the one below (also called 'long barrows').

Chamber

A hollow recess or room within a burial **mound**. The illustration below shows a cross-section of a **barrow** containing four chambers.

Fogou

The Cornish term for a **chamber**.

Mound

A rounded heap of soil or rocks, often (but not always) covering a burial **chamber**.

Dolmen

A tomb with one large rock (the **capstone**) perched on top of a number of vertical stones, like a rudimentary house. Different regions have their own names for the same structure (see overleaf).

Quoit
The Cornish term for a **dolmen**.

Cromlech
The Welsh term for a **dolmen**.

Earthwork
A large, purposefully constructed solid bank of soil, often used as the basis of stone monuments or for defensive purposes.

Henge
A round or oval **earthwork** consisting of a ring-shaped bank and ditch surrounding a central circular area. There might be a stone circle on this central platform, though note that the henge doesn't refer to the circle itself – a common misconception usually derived from the fact that Stonehenge is the best-known example.

Hillfort
A defensive structure typical to the Iron Age, where the hilltop is enclosed by a system of defensive soil banks and ditches (**earthworks**).

Cairn

A burial **mound** made of rocks (instead of soil). There might be a **chamber** inside.

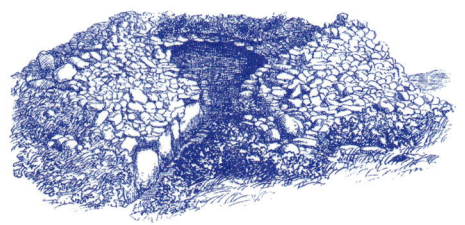

Cist grave

A small, coffin-like box tomb lined with rectangular stones.

A Note on Chalk Figures

This book contains a few examples of grand images carved into England's chalky downland. This traditional art form has largely (literally) faded over time, as millennia of scouring and cleaning is necessary to keep the things visible. Those chosen – the White Horse of Uffington (p.104) and the two figures of Cerne Abbas (p.26) and Wilmington (p.106) – might seem a paltry selection, given that there are around 50 chalk figures in Britain, mostly in the south. So, it seems appropriate to note here that most of those others existing today are modern creations merely in thrall to older versions of the form.

The eight White Horses of Wiltshire are the best examples of these: gleaming steeds hacked into the county's hillsides, the oldest of which, at Westbury, dates back to 1778 (and the newest, above Devises, to 1999). Even then, the origins of the two giants at Cerne Abbas and Wilmington – being vaguely mooted to the 10th and 7th centuries CE – do somewhat contradict the 'ancient' remit of this book, though their cryptic forms and scale are very much within the spirit of the thing.

Getting There

Most of the places in this book can be reached easily by car, though some require a short walk from the nearest parking spot. A handful are within easy walking distance from train stations, though most will require longer hikes, cycles or local buses if you are travelling without a car. You can use an app like AllTrails to plan a walking route. We also recommend researching each site before visiting, as more detailed travel information is available via the National Trust, English Heritage and other local tourism websites.

what3words

What3words uses a tag of three unique words to identify a precise 3-metre-square location. We have given the w3w tag for every place in this book (as opposed to GPS or Ordnance Survey coordinates), and they are especially helpful for pin-pointing the exact location of sites in remote areas. w3w is free and can be used online or via the app. Simply search using the three words, and then use a navigation app of your choice to plan a route.

Stonehenge, the most-visited megalithic site in the UK (p.32).
Opposite: Wistman's Wood, Devon's ancient temperate rainforest (p.62).

Castlerigg stone circle in Cumbria – one of the first ancient monuments to be taken into state guardianship in 1833 (p.114).

People gather at Avebury (p. 50) to celebrate the Summer Solstice.
Opposite: Pentre Ifan, Pembrokeshire's most famous dolmen (p. 158).

Southwest England

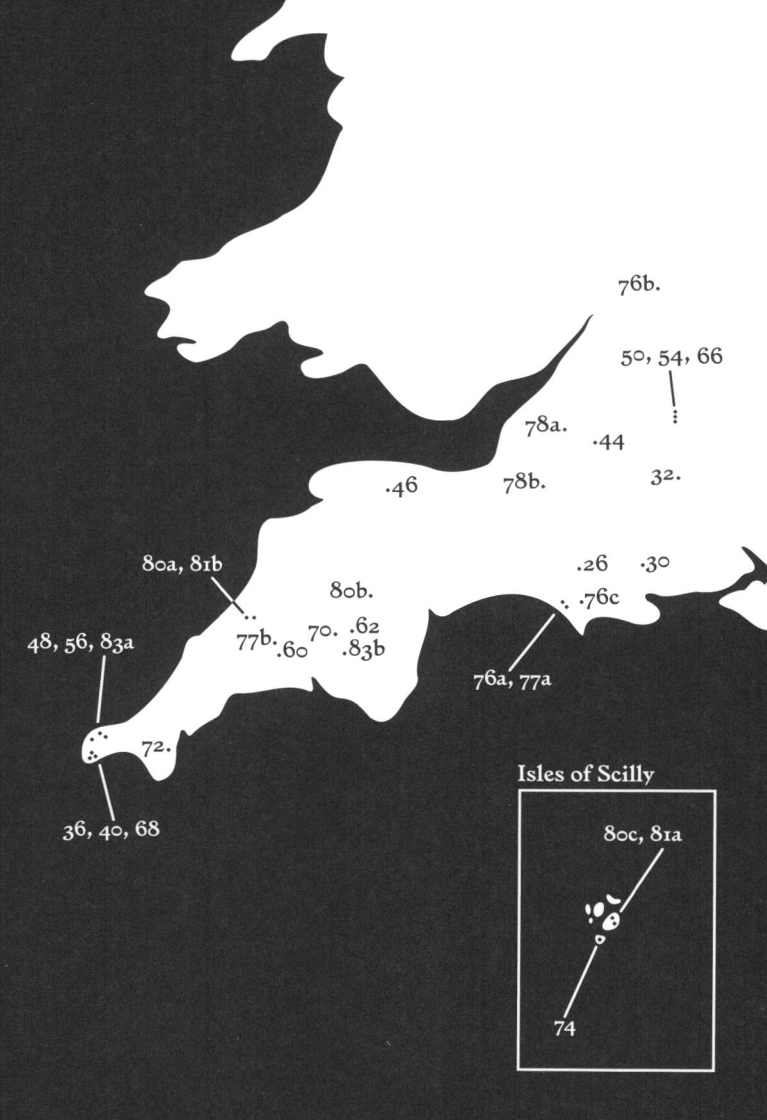

76b.

5o, 54, 66

78a.

.44

32.

.46

78b.

80a, 81b

80b.

.26 .3o

.76c

48, 56, 83a

77b. .60 70. .62
              .83b

76a, 77a

36, 40, 68

72.

Isles of Scilly

8oc, 81a

74

Cerne Abbas Giant

Phallic chalk figure cut into a hill

Dorset's over-excited colossus is one of the south's most winsomely idiosyncratic (and undeniably horny) fertility symbols. His roughly naturalistic proportions are huge: 55 metres tall, with a heavily knobbed club of 37 metres in his right hand, and a resplendent 9-metre phallus. The period of its creation is vague, but analysis by the National Trust in 2021 deduced it was probably Late Saxon (850–1066 CE).

What *is* widely concurred is the admirable effort employed by the local populace over the course of 1,500 years to protect the giant from both elements and turf. As noted by 20th-century archaeologist Jaquetta Hawkes, it's 'astonishing' that there was such a sustained effort to conserve the giant, given that his unashamedly Pagan symbolism would have been an affront to the locals' Christianity. An Iron Age earthwork called the 'Trendle' sits just to the north, where Morris Dancers continue to make merry every May Day.

Cerne Abbas, Dorset, DT2 7AL
Gentle 0.5KM walk from village centre; parking in village
///hypocrite.strutting.unsettled

Volunteers scrubbing the chalk of the Cerne Abbas Giant to keep the figure visible.

Badbury Rings

Three-ringed hillfort with a clumpy copse

The concentric marvel of Badbury Rings is a fortification of some prestige. A triple-ringed construction of Iron Age origin (though the site is thought to have supported some kind of anthropological action back to the Bronze Age), the spindly outer ring encases two massive inner ramparts (defensive walls) and ditches, sometimes thought reminiscent of Pagan turf mazes. Dual east and west entrances emphasise the likelihood of spiritual rather than defensive use, and there is an atmospheric pine-topped hill at its centre.

Nineteenth-century antiquarians reckoned the Rings were the Mount Badon of Arthurian lore (a guess based purely on the similar names), where King Arthur is said to have defeated the Saxons in 518 CE. A 1968 edition of *Dorset Magazine* also wrote of a 'ghostly cavalcade' of knights appearing at the Rings at midnight, and Arthur is said to appear as a spectral raven, 'croaking his satisfaction of the scene of his triumph' on the anniversary of the battle.

Blandford Road, Shapwick, Wimborne, Dorset, DT11 9JL
Parking on site
///parting.melts.threaded

Neolithic and Bronze Age

Stonehenge

The prehistoric world's most famous site

Where to start with Stonehenge, a place riveted into the psyche of anyone with even an infinitesimal interest in the mists of the ancient? Indeed, Henry of Huntingdon, writing around 1130, described the conglomeration of rocks, reaching 4 metres into the air above Salisbury Plain, as the second wonder of Britain (incongruously behind Wookey Hole, Somerset's limestone caves). It is a place suffused with mystery, having perplexed archaeologists for aeons, though it's now pretty widely accepted that it was likely built as a ceremonial temple aligned with the sun.

Prosaically, it's a collection of circles aligned towards sunrise and sunset on the Summer and Winter Solstices, respectively. Inside the main gargantuan ring is a second circle of smaller stones (commonly referred to as 'bluestones', a catch-all term for rocks transported to the region from far afield); inside this is a host of trilithons – pairs of upright stones with another (called a 'lintel') laid across the top. There is a large solitary stone (called the 'heel stone') to the distant northeast of the main circles.

Stonehenge's formation came in stages, starting around 3000 BCE. Following the initial Earthwork Phase – wherein an earthen henge and myriad chalk pits appeared – came the Bluestone Phase. Here, huge stones weighing up to ▶

4 tonnes were carted 150 miles from the Preseli Hills of southwest Wales and arranged in a central double circle. Recent research has found that the largest central rock – a partially buried altar stone – actually came from 435 miles away in Scotland, a lunatic feat of determination. Around 2400 BCE, 20-tonne sarsens (a kind of silicified sandstone carved from the Marlborough Downs) were positioned in circular and horse-shoe shapes, and the instantly recognisable lintels placed on top. That's the potted version of the story, but there's plenty more to dig into at the site's visitor centre (a rare boon in the world of ancient rocks, testament to Stonehenge's importance).

Further nuance abounds, but it remains a stupefying place – a project of unimaginable logistics whose celestial and solar composition, and possibly healing properties, are purported to have attracted thousands of pilgrims from all over Europe in its heyday. (Tooth analysis at the site has identified visitors from as far afield as Bavaria and the Mediterranean.)

Stonehenge remains a site of unparalleled antiquarian, countercultural and touristic heft, and there's simply no British experience quite like slowly rubbernecking the great temple in a traffic jam on the A303, blasting out the Spinal Tap banger dedicated to it. ('STONEHENGE! / WHERE THE DEMONS DWELL! / WHERE THE BANSHEES LIVE AND THEY DO LIVE WELL!' etc.)

Salisbury, Wiltshire, SP4 7DE
Parking on site, or bus from Salisbury station (19KM)
///awaited.passively.landings

Bronze Age

Boscawen-Un

Diminutive ring with a slanting centrepoint

Within a hedged enclosure and far from civilisation, this ring is one of West Penwith's most impactful sites. At the circle's centre is a rock set at a dramatic 45-degree angle – who knows whether this is an intentional design feature or the result of millennia of ageing. To the southwest of the circle is a large chunk of quartz, considered a symbol of femininity in hokey crystology circles. Here, it may have marked the position of the rising moon during the Summer Solstice, or perhaps a backsight for taking in sunrise on May Day. Speculation around solar alignment also abounds: the 19 ring stones could be a rounded-up representation of the Moon's 18.6-year 'lunar standstill cycle' – the time at which the northernmost and southernmost moonrise and moonset appear furthest apart. The place's significance has transcended the ages, too: Gorsedh Kernow (an organisation celebrating Cornwall's Celtic spirit) was inaugurated here in 1928.

Off the A30 near St. Buryan, Penzance, Cornwall, TR19 6EJ
Parking 0.8KM walk away in lay-by on A30
///pesky.stacks.types

The wonderful circle at Boscawen-Un sits within some of West Cornwall's prettiest tracts.

Carn Euny

Ancient village with an eerie fogou

Discovered by tin miners in the 18th century, this ancient village – occupied from the Iron Age until the dog days of the Roman era – is one of the best preserved in England's Southwest. Particularly natty is its spectacularly dank, 20-metre fogou: a stone-walled, subterranean passage specific to west Cornwall. Cattle shed? Hidey hole? Elaborate pantry? All mooted, though *The Modern Antiquarian* author Julian Cope supposes that its unique, circular central chamber was some kind of steamy sweat lodge due to an incorporated recess for a fireplace. A 2024 *Guardian* piece describes a covering of 'goblin's gold' moss, so called because of the way it shines luminously in the dark but dulls in sunlight – the source of myriad tales of lustrous faerie treasure turning to dirt by morning.

Adorably, the site was 'excavated' by a teenage William Copeland Borlase (great great grandson of Cornish antiquarian Rev. William Borlase) in 1863, using explosives of indeterminate origin. Boys will be boys.

Sancreed, Penzance, Cornwall, TR20 8RB
Parking on site
///village.riches.ambitions

The entrance to the 20-metre fogou.
Opposite: Ruined remains of the Carn Euny Iron Age settlement.

Neolithic

Stoney Littleton

Painterly, many-chambered tomb

It's a textbook example of a Neolithic chambered barrow, but Stoney Littleton's nattiest detail lies in the fossilised ammonite in the left-hand door jamb – a crossing of the geologic and anthropologic ages that appears as surreally out-of-place now as it must have then. The locale – an uphill schlep above Somerset's undulating levels, open to an enormous West Country sky – and low-slung appearance of the hump gives a furtive vibe, while crouching under the giant lintel into its damp, shadowy tunnels is an essential immersion for the budding antiquarian. An 1816 excavation located a bevy of old bones – but it's thought that earlier looters had already dealt with any spoils, granted unofficial access via a hole in the barrow created by an 18th-century farmer nicking stones for road-mending. It was restored properly in 1958; a mouldering plaque commemorates the project.

Wellow, Somerset, BA2 8NR
*Parking 0.5*KM *away at Littleton Lane*
///*tentacles.sourced.wished*

Iron Age

Cow Castle

Resplendent hillfort in a lonely locale

Located at the meeting of the rivers Barle and White Water, in a silent and sequestered spot in Exmoor National Park, Cow Castle is a precipitous hill fort renowned for its melancholy beauty and vertiginously steep sides. It's oval-shaped, with a sole rampart and a second entrance at its southwest side, marked by a diminutive standing stone. Cow Castle is said to have been built by faeries to protect some resident earth spirits (or by men for a still undetermined purpose of defence, as a sanctuary or as a haven for cattle). Whatever the intent, it's a perfect example of the form, its low-key haunting cache only bolstered by the lengthy 3-kilometre (but quite manageable, terrain-wise) walk from the nearest car park and loos.

Exmoor National Park, Somerset, TA24 7JT
Parking 3 KM away in Simonsbath village
///emphasis.pacifist.trek

Neolithic

Lanyon Quoit

Exemplary dolmen re-erected in the 1800s

A bona fide Cornish icon, this picture-perfect dolmen table nevertheless drew shade from pioneering archaeologist and sass-queen Jacquetta Hawkes, who noted that, situated in striking distance from Penzance 'where, seasonally, there are many people with not enough to do, it is one of the most visited monuments in the West Country'. Harsh. But IRL it's a vision: three granite uprights, each 1.5 metres tall, with a gargantuan, 13-tonne capstone and various other slabs buried nearby. The aforementioned 18th-century antiquarian Rev. William Borlase surveyed the site, noting a neater original construction – with a capstone high enough that a man could sit on horseback beneath it – but one of the supports and the horizontal table-stone fell in an 1815 gale. In a kind of proto-Kickstarter, local folk funded its repair in 1824, led by a helpful Royal Navy captain.

Northeast of Madron, Penzance, Cornwall, TR20 8NY
Parking 1.5KM away at Daytime Car Park, near Mên-an-Tol
///chain.decanter.spins

Neolithic and Bronze Age

Avebury

The blinding, haunting exemplar of an ancient site

The big one: Avebury is the full esoteric caboodle, and even acknowledging the steely splendour of Stonehenge (p.32) rising from Salisbury Plain, the country's most awesome ancient assemblage. (Writing around 1663, antiquary John Aubrey claimed that Avebury 'does as much exceed in greatness the so renowned Stonehenge, as a cathedral does a parish church'; given the scope and inscrutable mystic fervour of the place, on a crystalline autumn day, it's hard to disagree.)

It's a leviathan complex of stone rings, geometric avenues and earthworks running towards, through and around the eponymous village, over 1,280 metres in overall circumference. A massive henge ditch encloses around 11 hectares of land, and within this lies the world's greatest stone circle (now 27 stones, but once around 100, before the majority were removed by superstitious medieval types and those in need of building supplies), plus two smaller circles. Similarly head-razing is the length of West Kennet Avenue: a 2.4-kilometre byway marked by 100 pairs of stones with an average height of 3 metres, leading rovers ancient and modern to a now-vanished circle called the 'Sanctuary', destroyed by farmers in the 1700s so the land could be appropriated for agriculture. ▶

*The wider site of Avebury includes Britain's largest stone circle,
with a diameter of over 300 metres.*

The site was cleared of foliage and restored in the 1930s by archaeologist Andrew Keiller (who found the bones of a 'barber surgeon' in the process: a godly and itinerant medieval medicine man crushed when a megalith he was trying to bury collapsed on top of him in the 1320s). The landscape here thrums with an undeniable otherworldly energy, a fact embraced by a raft of cultural curios referencing it over the years – whether Derek Jarman's woozily radiant 1971 short film *A Journey to Avebury*, or 1978's bizarre teatime fantasy drama *Children of the Stones*.

Despite its preposterous size and obvious historical significance, the actual purpose of Avebury remains unknown. It was likely ritualistic or ceremonial, or perhaps a place for communities to gather for seasonal festivities (though the scarcity of prehistoric litter like pottery and bone shards within the henge itself suggest it might have been out of bounds for the plebs). But visiting now, millennia upon millennia later, the place remains spellbinding. Avebury's Red Lion pub boasts an extra heady ambience, though whether that's down to its location literally within the bounds of the stone circle or the trough-loads of local ale you've just quaffed is up for debate…

Marlborough, Wiltshire, SN8 1RF
Parking on site
///heckler.facing.mole

Neolithic

Silbury Hill

Europe's superlative man-made mound

Riveting as Avebury (p.50) is, the oversized pudding of Silbury Hill nearby is equally eye-popping, rising nearly 40 metres from flat grassland. Constructed piecemeal between around 2400–2300 BCE, this is the tallest prehistoric man-made mound in Europe. Analysis of the labour required to construct such a thing without industrial-scale tools reckons 18 million man-hours: that's 500 men toiling for 15 years to fashion an ascetic dome of enigmatic function. The interior is chalk, suggesting it would have been entirely white on completion: the ghost of a hill. Legends suppose it was the resting place of the Neolithic ruler King Sil or that it's the remnants of a great sack of soil the Devil had intended to drop on the populace of nearby Marlborough. Notions of ritual and burial use abound, but, as with most other locations in this book, it's still a mystery. James Dyer, author of 1973's indispensable *Southern England: An Archaeological Guide*, claims the flat top was once used as a cricket pitch. Fielding must have been a nightmare.

West Kennet, Marlborough, Wiltshire, SN8 1QH
Parking on site
///sprinting.tilts.tender

Late Neolithic or early Bronze Age

Mên-an-Tol

West Penwith's giant stone doughnut

An overarching air of mystery prevails over West Cornwall's most diminutively otherworldly site. Located off a long, gorse-lined track deep into the Penwith moor, it consists of a short line of two upright stones and a round (actually slightly octagonal) one between them, with the centre holed out like a giant rock doughnut. It's unlikely they were always set out this way: a 1749 survey by William Borlase suggested a triangular formation, while a 1993 report by the Cornwall Historic Environment Service thought it more likely that the rocks were taken at some juncture from a bigger circle of 20 or so and repositioned here.

Referred to as 'the wind's vagina' by oddball Cornish poet DM Thomas (each to their own), it remains a place brimming with folklore, much to do with healing and fertility. Most tales involve someone clambering or being passed through the central O-stone: farmers to cure bad backs; women to improve fertility; ill children to rid themselves of rickets; or changeling babies (grotesque and witless infants, switched for a human child by their faerie guardian) to be transformed back into mortal bairns. The 19th–20th century astronomer Norman Lockyer even claimed the stones were a functioning oracle. He suggested that two pins placed in a cross shape on the central rock might ▶

start shifting around in a 'peculiar motion', which could be interpreted to answer pressing questions ('Where did I leave my keys?' for instance). In any case, Julian Cope rightly described the magic here as 'deep and severe' – the gravity of which, admittedly, depends on the inclemency of the always changeable Penwith weather.

Mên-an-Tol isn't alone in Penwith's austere landscape. Around 300 metres to the north is Mên Scryfa: a 1.7-metre rock, probably Bronze Age and inscribed with the message 'Rialobrani Cunovali fil', or 'Rialobranus son of Cunovalus' – a neat bit of Anglo Saxon-era graffiti possibly referring to a local pre-Roman Cornish king or tribal leader who may also have died in battle nearby.

East of Morvah, Penzance, Cornwall, TR20 8NU
Parking 1KM away at Daytime Car Park
///printouts.callers.cracking

Trevethy Quoit

Grand chamber with a mysterious borehole

This is one of the more incongruously placed quoits (upright stone tombs) in Cornwall, found in the hamlet of Tremar Coombe on the edge of Bodmin Moor and basically in someone's garden (as a quick snoop on Google Maps' Street View will attest). But Trevethy is nonetheless one of the Southwest's finest Neolithic chambers. Its 2.5-metre stones – five in number – and maniacally large 18-tonne capstone more than deserve the local nickname of the 'Giant's House'. Incidentally, *that* name probably comes from the writing of a 16th-century antiquarian called John Norden, who described it as a rather winsome 'little howse raised of mightie stones' (albeit an abode for the expired, being a tomb). A tiny, notched hole in one corner of the slanted cap gives extra mystery: the jury's out on whether it was bored in for some astronomical purpose or simply the neat byproduct of four millenniums' weathering.

Off the B3254, near Darite, Liskeard, Cornwall, PL14 5JY
Parking on site
///scorch.muted.slimy

Wistman's Wood

Haunted prehistoric woodland

Wistman's oldest trees are only ('only') 500 years old, but this tract of high-altitude wood is one of Britain's last clumps of ancient temperate rainforest, and thus worthy of inclusion here. In fact, woodland of this kind would have covered Dartmoor for millennia, before being cleared by Neolithic farmers for agricultural and hunting use, making Wistman's a truly authentic vision of a long-bygone age.

The abnormal atmosphere is palpable: three hectares of mainly dwarf oak, gnarled branches covered in moss and lichen, contorting around and over a floor of equally carpeted boulders. It's all hugely spooky (plus overflowing with adders) and linked to various ghostly tales. Some tell of druids performing esoteric rites over rocks carved with spirals and other odd symbols, or on the still-surviving Druid's (or Altar) Stone – a rock said to occasionally be found flecked with ritualistic animal blood.

Another is that it is the home of a pack of hellhounds who reside among the boulders and roots, occasionally taking off across the moor with a huge huntsman, tooting a giant horn and seeking out unfortunate wanderers. The whole group together comprises something called the 'Wild Hunt', variations of which appear in the folklore of several European societies. The name 'Wistman', appropriately, ▶

derives from a Devonshire parlance for 'eerie'. It's all certainly worth a dose of the willies.

Visitors must tread with caution – Wistman's Wood is a delicate ecosystem and, while its boulders, branches and mosses may appear rugged, they're really rather fragile (and, in the case of the Horsehair lichen that makes its home here, incredibly rare). The wood can be circled on foot, but it's now prohibited to enter – a conservational necessity that, if anything, makes peering into its green-carpeted depths even more uncanny.

More tangibly, human history survives in these parts, as well – the woods are surrounded by the ruined remnants of over 100 Bronze Age huts.

Two Bridges, Princetown, Devon, PL20 6SW
Parking opposite the Two Bridges Hotel
///stoppage.interviewer.lows

West Kennet Long Barrow

Looming tomb near Avebury

West Kennet Long Barrow is yet more gold in Avebury's arcadian rural landscape. This whacking great Neolithic tomb is a whopper: more than 100 metres long and 2.4 metres high (one of the largest of its kind in England). It was constructed around 3650 BCE as a burial chamber and around 46 bodies were interred over 30 years – as evidenced by the abundance of ritualistic grave goods, bits of primaeval detritus and bones smashed shaman-style against the walls. After this, the chambers were filled to the rafters with stone and earth. Once a chalky white exterior, its portal stones now precede a tufty grass mound, the main passage of which stretches 13 metres into the ground. Ambling the chilly tunnels and tombs is disquieting as is, but err away on Midsummer's Day, when legend suggests that it's also visited by a ghostly priest and a large white hound.

West Kennett, Marlborough, Wiltshire, SN8 1QH
Parking 0.8KM walk away in lay-by signposted on A4
///albums.painters.rarely

The Merry Maidens

A perfect stone circle with lofty neighbours

One of Land's End's more breezily accessible monuments – being easy ambling distance from the South West Coast Path *and* smack-bang next to a stop for the open-top Coaster bus – the Maidens is an exquisite 19-stone ring in a gentle Arcadian meadow. The road itself hacks straight through the ruined cairn chamber of Tregiffian, dotted with cup marks. Also nearby are two vertiginous, phallic megaliths dubbed 'the Pipers'. Legend has it that the collective was once a human party, whooping it up on a Saturday evening. As a clock striking midnight rang out in the nearby village of St. Buryan, the Pipers fled, leaving the Maidens dancing past the Sabbath. The latter were thus turned to stone as punishment for their heathen jigging, the former for cowardly hoofing it from the scene of the crime. Men!

3 km southeast of St. Buryan on the B3315,
Penzance, TR19 6BQ
Parking on site
///pounding.cocoons.evenings

Merrivale Stone Rows

Extensive rock lines with a sickly history

There are a cool 86 stone rows strung about Dartmoor's wind-whipped uplands, yet no one really has the foggiest why they're there. But those comprising the Merrivale complex – two double rows of 200 stones and a nearby single one of six, plus a few other small lines and a stone circle – are located in such proximity to various funerary cairns, a trace of a barrow and box-like stone cist graves that common sense assumes ritual purpose.

Still, recent history is more putrid. The rows are colloquially known as the Plague Market because in 1625, during an outbreak of the bubonic plague in the town of Tavistock, farmers would leave food on the stones for the stricken, who would switch them for cash. These days, the dinky stature of the rocks gives a Richard Long-esque Land Art flavour to the scene.

Merrivale, Princetown, Yelverton, Devon, PL20 6ST
Parking on site
///inflation.frocks.canny

Halliggye Fogou

Superbly preserved subterranean tunnel

Etymologically, the word 'fogou' (a kind of underground chamber network specific to Cornwall) is derived from the Cornish 'ogo', for 'cave' – evoking the murky, den-like appeal of these little-known passages. Buried within the historic Trelowarren Estate on the banks of the Lizard Peninsula's languid Helford River, Halligye is an eminent example. It's a shadowy construction of sunken slabs accessed via modern steps, with a long main passage that becomes a more stooping 'creep' (i.e. a passage with a notably lower ceiling) at its far end, with a gently meandering tunnel swooping to the left from it (plus a later, probably exploratory entrance knocked into it around halfway along). As with Carn Euny (p.40), the purpose of the fogou is obscure, but a raised 'stumbling block' built into the floor – designed to trip up would-be intruders – means it may have been built as a hiding place or for storage. Take a torch and avoid visiting entirely from October to April, when it becomes a home for roosting bats.

Trelowarren Estate, St. Mawgan, Helston, Cornwall, TR12 6AF
Parking on site
///tone.random.worms

Old Man of Gugh

A sole Scillonian seaside megalith

Miniscule in size but mammoth in ancient heft, the Scilly isle of Gugh (and the larger St. Agnes, to which it's connected by a strip of sand at low tide) might be the most alluring outcrop in this already enchanting archipelago. It's basically two heath-covered hills with a couple of houses in between. The undulating humps are pockmarked with cairns, tombs and cist graves – not least Obadiah's Barrow, a somewhat tumbledown chamber still worth the hillside scramble.

The de facto nucleus is this, a 2.7-metre menhir, tilting finger-like towards the water between Gugh and the 'main' island of St. Mary's. The earth around the stone was excavated in 1900 with zero spoils (though the island has generally thrown up very few finds, possibly due to the degrading effects of its acidic soil).

Gugh, Scilly Isles, TR22 0PL
Ferry to St. Agnes from St. Mary's (Scilly's main isle)
and walk across sandbank at low tide
///fictional.luckier.cork

Neolithic
The Hell Stone, Dorset

This squat, crab-like Neolithic dolmen table is found at the far end of a poorly restored 24-metre mound on Portesham Hill in Dorset. Having collapsed at some point in its long history, the Hell Stone was sloppily re-erected in the 1860s, its stones standing in a slipshod rather than geometric shape. The name isn't actually infernal: it's a riff on the Old English 'heelstone', meaning to conceal, in reference to the capstone.

Portesham, Weymouth, DT3 4EY
///hardens.victor.agreement

Neolithic
Belas Knap, Gloucestershire

Located near Cheltenham, this immaculate long barrow features side chambers, some very elaborate stone walling and a sneaky false entrance. It is considered one of the finest of the regional group of Cotswold-Severn barrows defined by archaeologist Glyn Daniel.

Winchcombe, Cheltenham, GL54 5AL
///withdraws.fortunate.widest

Iron Age
Maiden Castle, Dorset

The Iron Age hillfort to rule them all, Maiden Castle, near Dorchester, is a wildly undulating series of hilltop crevices and ramparts, and the most complex site of its ilk in Britain. The ditches are immense, and there's a bevy of supplementary burial mounds on the right-hand side.

Maiden Castle Road, Dorchester, DT2 9PP
///immediate.mailing.retained

Bronze Age
Winterbourne Poor Lot Barrows, Dorset

Dotted just off the A35 near Winterbourne Abbas, this cemetery complex of 44 Bronze Age burial barrows (convex 'bowl', concave 'pond' and flat 'disc' variations among them) is curious for the fact of being in a valley rather than on top of a hill (as was the standard ancient want, given their occasional use as territorial totems).

Winterbourne Abbas, Dorchester, DT2 9XD
///blown.promise.afraid

Bronze Age
The Hurlers, Cornwall

There's extra bang for your ancient buck here: three stone circles arranged in a line, a grouping unseen elsewhere in England, and the finest ceremonial rings in the Southwest. Like the Merry Maidens (p.68), religious transgression made them – in this case, frivolous men doing something as reckless as playing hurling on the sabbath.

Minions, Liskeard, PL14 5LE
///aunts.hitters.swear

Late Neolithic or early Bronze Age

Stanton Drew, Somerset

The third biggest complex of standing stones in England – located in the titular Somerset village – is also one of its more mysterious. This mishmash comprises the Great Circle (of 26 stones, 113 metres across), a group of three mismatching rocks called the Cove (in the village pub's garden) and, 500 metres away, a fallen slab called Hautville's Quoit. The seemingly random layout has perplexed antiquarians for aeons, though many now believe they were part of a much more elaborate ritual landscape, now vanished.

Stanton Drew, BS39 4EW
///powerful.twitching.dripped

Prehistoric

Glastonbury Tor, Somerset

It's not man-made, but this lofty knoll topped with a 15th-century church tower is integral to Celtic, Pagan and Arthurian history and myth, as well as standing over the crossing of the Michael and Mary Ley lines (imaginary paths running between ancient sites or sacred hills, believed by some to channel natural and psychic energies). Visit on May Day to witness the Glastonbury Order of Druids hosting their Beltane celebrations (an ancient Celtic fertility rite complete with Morris dancing, blessings and a May Pole).

Glastonbury Tor, Glastonbury, BA6 8BG
///joys.loads.bidder

Spinster's Rock, Devon's textbook dolmen (overleaf).

Late Neolithic or early Bronze Age
Stannon Stone Circle, Cornwall

It's remote, alright – plonked on Dinnever Hill in the north-west of Bodmin Moor, hence the limited address info – but Stannon's 80-ish granite chunks are worth the hike. Take in the stylistic similarities with the large-scale and comparative rings found in distant Cumbria (bolstering the idea that itinerant ring-builders might have travelled south to show off their skills).

Near Highertown on Bodmin Moor, PL32 9QA
///sounding.variety.perplexed

Neolithic
Spinster's Rock, Devon

This is Devon's textbook dolmen, located off a small road heading to Drewsteignton. The three neat uprights and a rounded capstone are named in thrall to three bored spinsters who are said to have erected the tomb as a way to kill time before breakfast. Beats an early HIIT class.

1 Shilstone Cottages, Chagford, Newton Abbot, TQ13 8JX
///eager.conjured.lessening

Bronze Age
Giant's Grave, Cornwall

Innisidgen is a scheduled Bronze Age complex on St. Mary's, and the Giant's Grave (sometimes called 'Upper Innisidgen') its star attraction. A picture-perfect and perplexingly well-preserved turf-topped entrance grave (a chamber tomb under a mound, with a stone-lined passage at its fore), its shadowy depths are earthen catnip for any budding Bronze Age snoops.

St. Mary's, Isles of Scilly, TR21 0NX
///recount.scaffold.providing

Bronze Age
Porth Hellick Down, Cornwall

Along with the Giant's Grave, this is the Scilly Isles' *other* ripper entrance grave. Port Hellick's USP might be the oversized jamb that almost blocks its entrance portal (though the panorama of the Celtic Sea comes a close second).

St. Mary's, Isles of Scilly, TR21 0NY
///venturing.flight.downcast

Bronze Age
Brown Willy Cairns, Cornwall

Cornwall's loftiest hill (at 420 metres above sea level), Brown Willy occupies a bleak spot on Bodmin Moor. At its summit is a large Bronze Age cairn, occasionally believed to be the grave of a bygone Cornish king and now a holy site of pilgrimage for followers of the New Age Aetherius Society – a UFO- and yoga-obsessed new religious movement.

Brown Willy, Camelford, PL30 4PQ
///author.montage.genius

Ballowall Barrow, a Bronze Age funerary monument on the Cornish coast.

Bronze Age
Ballowall Barrow, Cornwall

A globular, robust barrow, Ballowall is situated on the far West Penwith coast among the scarred remnants of the region's tin-mining history (and, until its discovery in 1878, hidden by mining debris). Now, its fine form is open to the elements, with a dramatic aspect of the east Atlantic.

St. Just, Penzance, TR19 7NP
///awaiting.blotting.decking

Bronze Age
Yellowmead Stone Circle, Cornwall

Unearthed in 1921 (after a fire singed off much of the heather that had subsumed the rocks for years), Yellowmead comprises four concentric rings, one inside another. The name's a misnomer: it was once recorded as Hollemede, but the H is silent – 'Ollemede' meaning 'old meadowland'.

Sheepstor, Yelverton, PL20 6PF
///dizziness.name.cyber

Southeast, Central
and Eastern England

106.

.86

·94

92.·102

108a. .90
108b ·110a

·108c

98.   104
              ·

·.88

110b

Neolithic

Arthur's Stone, Herefordshire

Gargantuan chamber above the Golden Valley

Sat in the hills, with a distant aspect of the Black Mountains and the holy Skirrid over the Welsh border, Arthur's Stone is a heaving chamber tomb formed of nine upright slabs and a huge, 20+ tonne capstone roof, now split in two. The name derives from the notion that King Arthur killed a giant here, whose elbows dented a nearby slab as he fell. The tomb is also positioned on a confluence of three Ley lines (straight, spectral pathways supposedly connecting natural and prehistoric sites significant to ancient peoples). Weirdly, a fruity local story recorded by the Rev. Francis Kilvert suggested the stone was shrinking (rather than growing, which is another fairly frequent event in stone lore for some reason). Whatever the truth of it, the aura is irrefutable.

Arthur's Stone Lane, Dorstone,
Hereford, Herefordshire, HR3 6AX
Parking on site or 2KM away in Dorstone village
///snapper.weds.endearing

Neolithic

Mottistone Longstone

A looming menhir with wild coastal views

The Isle of Wight's ancient landscape is an immersive timeslip of wooded barrows and mounds, with Mottistone Longstone its imposing heart. Sat at the foot of the Iron Age fort of Castle Hill, on a ridge overlooking the Channel's shining reflection, Mottisone consists of a rising vertical megalith and recumbent neighbour. Legend has it that the stones were propelled into place in a contest between Saint Catherine (a martyred 4th-century virgin and important late medieval saint, also commemorated in the names of a nearby downs and lighthouse) and the Devil, who threw them from a hillside to the east, with Lucifer's smaller stone falling short. This is a caper, but the rocks *are*, in fact, remnants of a 60,000-year-old Neolithic barrow stretching 31 metres east to west. They were also the possible site of sky burials, wherein corpses were left to be stripped by hungry fauna, the bones then interred.

Next to Longstone Cottage, Strawberry Lane,
Mottistone, Isle of Wight, PO30 4EB
Parking 1KM away off Strawberry Lane, PO30 4EA
///applies.lushly.assure

Kit's Coty House

Grand dolmen chamber in the Kent countryside

Despite a scathing review in James Dyer's 1973 classic *Southern England: An Archaeological Guide* – 'Something of a disappointment. The great stones of the burial chamber are herded together in a hideous iron fence as though to prevent their escape' – Kit's Coty House is Kent's preeminent ancient site. Three upright stones are arranged in an H-shape as a 'false portal': a decoy entrance designed to confuse thieves (also sometimes interpreted as a 'spirit door', with the alternative function of letting in the dead). One legend tells that the titular Kit was Catigern, who fought Horsa in 455 CE and was buried here (phantasmic reenactments are said to take place); others posit that he was a lowly shepherd who cowered from the elements in the tomb. Either way, the name is a tautology; 'cote' is a small house in Old English. Nearby lies Little Kit's Coty House, its supposedly 'countless' stones now a heap on the floor.

Off Chatham Road, Aylesford, Kent, ME20 7EZ
Parking and train station 4KM away in Aylesford village
///technical.freezing.mass

Neolithic

Wayland's Smithy

Mound with a spectral inhabitant

Set in a lonely beech grove high off the Ridgeway path, above the Vale of the White Horse, this giant tomb was built in two stages. The original part was a mortuary house: a chamber of stone and wood, where the bodies of 14 people were holed up, then covered with earth and chalk. Years later, this extant, magnificent amalgam was constructed over the top of it: a 61-metre barrow across two low chambers, with four sarsens positioned like ageless guardians and a dinky entrance stone.

As for the nomenclature, the titular Wayland was a magical blacksmith with origins in Saxon and Norse mythology, captured by a king and lamed to stop him from fleeing. Local word has it that if one leaves a horse and a single groat (coin) outside the mound overnight, by morning, the animal will be shoed, and the cash disappeared.

West of the White Horse of Uffington along the Rigdeway
trail, near Ashbury, Oxfordshire, SN6 8BZ
Parking 1.6KM away at White Horse Hill, SN7 7QL
///obliging.replaying.kingpin

Rollright Stones

A trio of regal monuments near Chipping Norton

This is a witchy wonder of a Cotswold complex: three meg-alithic monuments assembled over 2,000 years between the Neolithic and Bronze Ages, constructed from boulders of Jurassic oolitic limestone mined some 500 metres away. The most popular folkloric origin story tells of a local king and his army met by a witch, who presented an irksome challenge of taking 'seven long strides' and trying to spot the local village of Long Compton.

'If thou canst see,' she said, 'King of England thou shalt be.' A good deal, but after seven strides, he could only see a nearby barrow, prompting the crone to declare: 'Thou and thy men hoar stones [a kind of ancient boundary-marking stone] shall be, and myself an eldern tree.' The king and his men were petrified, and the collective Rollrights formed.

First up, there are the King's Men: around 70 stones – famously 'uncountable', a trend in ancient rocks – in an asymmetric ring ('corroded like worm eaten wood, by the harsh Jaws of Time,' described 18th-century antiquarian William Stukeley). There's a portal entrance and two exterior rocks, close-set ring stones and a level interior: a style synonymous with some of the big-name Lake District complexes, which suggests the builders may have traipsed south to construct this one. ▶

The Whispering Knights, so-called because the upright stones are leaning in as if conspiring against the King.

The King's Men stone circle, part of the Rollright Stones complex.

Nearby are the Whispering Knights: an eerie dolmen chamber of four upright stones – all leaning in, supposedly a cabal of mutinous chevaliers conspiring against His Majesty – and a fallen capstone, with a portal facade facing downhill. It's a spectacle – possibly one of the country's first monuments memorialising the dead – with the pillar stone standing as the complex's heftiest.

Finally, the King Stone: up on the crest of a hill near a Bronze Age cairn and another barrow (probably a burial memorial rather than a clumsily removed outlier of the King's Men), its shape hewed down by centuries of souvenir hunters, soldiers and cattle drovers chipping bits off it for luck charms. What it lacks in adornments, it makes up for in subtext. One neat tale describes a man who used 24 horses to drag the stone to his house, causing dreadful noises to ring out, until he was compelled by the din to return it – which he managed, strangely, with just two horses. Another, posited by the aforementioned Stukely, tells of crowds gathering at Midsummer's Eve, cutting the witch's eldern tree and causing the King Stone to move its 'head'.

Rollright Road, Little Rollright, Chipping Norton,
Oxfordshire, OX7 5QB
Parking on site
///city.skylights.widgets

Cissbury Ring

The largest hillfort in Sussex

An awesome hilltop enclosure of 26 hectares enclosed in a ditch with a single rampart, Cissbury Ring is also the country's second-most lauded group of dimpled Neolithic flint mines (after Grime's Graves, p.108). The enclosure was built in 400 BCE, used as a defensive hub for around 300 years and thereafter for agriculture. After *that*, it was variously appropriated as a Roman settlement and coin mint; part of a Tudor beacon system; and as an anti-aircraft battery in the Second World War. A Victorian excavation threw up an inventory of the deer antler picks and ox shoulder shovels that were apparently used to dig out the original mine. Archaeologist Jacquetta Hawkes noted how ludicrous the build must have been given the primitive origins: a 'stupendous effort' driven by 'obsessional madness'.

Findon, Valley, Worthing, West Sussex, BN14 0HT
Parking on site, or 6KM walk from Worthing station
///enjoyable.vacancies.liquid

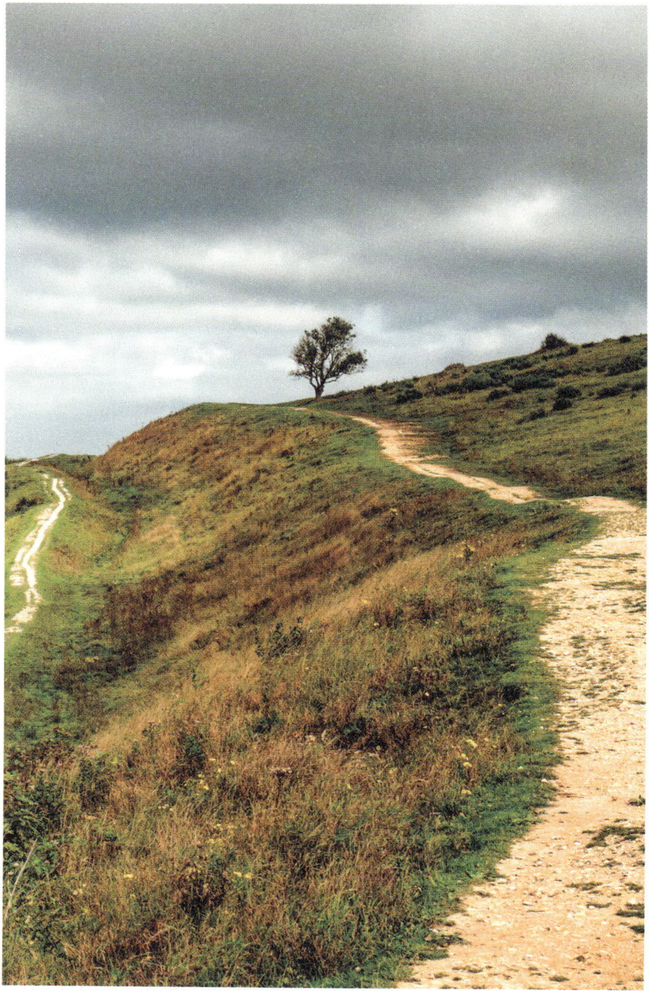

Cissbury Ring, the largest hillfort in Sussex.

White Horse of Uffington

Equine chalk figure on an eponymous hill

Unlike the south's proliferation of chalk horses, the equine icon of Uffington – the largest of all Britain's hill figures at 110 metres long and 40 metres high – is rendered in the abstract. A sweeping and idiomatic vision, as painterly as it is naive, it reflects the contours of the steep coombe hill into which it was carved. (The others, most of which are dotted across Wiltshire, are far sturdier and more straightforwardly 'horse-like' in design – see p.16 for more.)

As with the Cerne Abbas Giant (p.26), part of the wonderment stems from the sheer amount of upkeep the horse has demanded over the centuries. Testing ionising radiation levels in the sediment in the 1990s placed its creation between 1380 BCE and 550 BCE, and its chalk outline would have been scoured regularly since. In any case, the horse is an omnipresent image – not least as the cover for Swindon post-punk heroes XTC's 1982 *English Settlement* album.

Uffington, Oxfordshire, SN7 7UK
Parking on site
///registers.changed.soccer

Probably 7th century

Long Man of Wilmington

Mighty humanoid of mysterious origins

As obtuse in conception as the Cerne Abbas Giant (p.26) (if somewhat less lurid), the Long Man of Wilmington is an aesthetic anomaly in the world of chalk figures for its canny embrace of perspective. He's gargantuan: 70 metres tall, holding a pair of staves and with feet that buck the rest of the figure's symmetry, turning slightly to the east. Up close, the man looks distended and warped – it's only by viewing from a distance that he takes a conventional shape. He's variously been pinned as a fertility symbol, a massive skier or a Pagan image of Woden (the Old English name for the Norse god Odin). Another theory goes that his staves were demilitarised and the spear blades removed with the advent of Christianity. As is, he remains the unreadable icon of Sussex's verdant folds.

South Downs Way, Wilmington, Eastbourne, East Sussex, BN26 5QX
Parking 1.6KM away at Wilmington Priory, BN26 5SW
Polegate station 5.5KM away
///scar.marker.herb

Neolithic

Grime's Graves

Pockmarked meadow above an open flint mine

An astonishing expanse of undulating grassy dimples –
redolent of nothing less than a turf-covered lunar landscape,
an infestation of mega-moles or a dirt-biker's fever dream
– Grime's Graves comprises the remnants of 366 Neolithic
flint-mining pits, plus various other surveys and digs. They
were opened around 4,500 years ago to chip the dusky-
black stone for arrowheads, axes, myriad scraping tools
and ceremonial trinkets.

Ritual eeriness abounds, not least in Greenwell's Pit.
Named for the Victorian archaeologist Canon William
Greenwell, this is the oldest and deepest shaft to have been
explored and was found to contain a buried dog skeleton
– though no one knows why. Despite this, the morbid title
is a bit of a misnomer: the possessive, titular Grime (who is
he?) was long thought to be the creator, but 'Graves' simply
refers to hollows rather than anything more ailing.

Lynford, Thetford, Norfolk, IP26 5DE
Parking on site, or 5.5KM walk from Brandon station
///welfare.submits.lollipop

Neolithic
Coldrum Stones, Kent

Another classic Kentish long barrow and a superlative example of the region's Medway Megaliths (not least as, even at 6,000 years old and thus more grizzled than Stonehenge, it's still basically intact). Etymologically, it may link to the Cornish 'Galdrum', meaning 'place of enchantments'.

Trottiscliffe, West Malling, ME19 5EG
///stir.likely.hours

Neolithic
Addington Long Barrow, Kent

A spookily ruined chambered barrow near Addington, located on private land but perfectly visible from a lane that (unfortunately) cleaves straight through the middle of it. Its smashing was probably the result of either medieval treasure hunting or Christian iconoclasm.

Addington, West Malling, ME19 5BH
///cargo.apply.hits

Iron Age
Danebury Ring, Hampshire

These gigantic Iron Age earthworks and ramparts are surrounded by beech trees in a beatific downland setting near Stockbridge. The fort was heavily surveyed from 1969–88 – then the longest excavation of its kind in western Europe.

Stockbridge, SO20 6HZ
///blemishes.shippers.lovely

Coldrum Stones, one of the Medway Megaliths – a group of Neolithic monuments found in the lower valley of the River Medway, Kent.

Neolithic
Coffin Stone, Kent

A large, horizontal sarsen rock near Blue Bell Hill in Kent, topped with a slightly smaller rock that was placed by a farmer in 1980. A pair of skulls were found beneath it in 1836. Despite this, long-held theories that the stone was part of a burial barrow are considered defunct, the stone likely having been moved to this location in the medieval era.

Aylesford, ME20 7ED
///gift.clays.juror

Bronze Age
Brighstone Forest Barrows, Isle of Wight

The steep hills around the Longstone are dotted with mounds, but the trio of bell barrows in the depths of nearby Brighstone woods are unbeatably atmospheric (especially when looming into view through the trees on a mizzly, mist-covered winter morning).

Near Brighstone village, Newport, PO30 4AY
///pegs.slim.down

Danebury Ring, a gigantic Iron Age hillfort (previous page).

Northern England

132b.

.116

114.   .120

.122   128.

                132c.

                        .132a   126.

130b

                130c.

                124. .130a

Castlerigg

Spectacular stone circle and inspiration to Keats

It's little wonder the majestic stone circle of Castlerigg made a mark on the Romantic poet John Keats. His 1820 poem 'Hyperion' tells of 'Scarce images of life, one here, one there, / Lay vast and edgeways; like a dismal cirque / Of Druid stones, upon a forlorn moor'. Its sweeping setting – in a divine natural hippodrome formed by the Cumbrian peaks of Helvellyn, Skiddaw, Lonscale Fell, Blencathra, Clough Head and Derwent – is breathtaking.

The stones themselves are modest: 38 in total, ranging from one to 2.5 metres in height, with a diameter of around 30 metres. An ancillary rectangle of standing stones within the main ring is an idiosyncratic addition only seen once elsewhere (within another circle near Ullswater). As ever, origins are murky, but, being placed at around 3000 BCE, it's one of the oldest ancient monuments of its kind (and one of the first to be taken into state guardianship in 1833).

Castle Lane, Underskiddaw, Keswick, Cumbria, CA12 4RN
Parking on site, or 2.5KM walk from Keswick village
///deodorant.pinks.pounce

Northern England

Neolithic

Long Meg and Her Daughters

Circle with a saucy origin story

This is the third-widest stone circle in England (after Avebury, p.50, and Stanton Drew, p.78) and comes with more
Romantic kudos – this time from William Wordsworth. He
breathlessly noted that: 'I have not seen any other relique of
those dark ages which can pretend to rival it in singularity
and dignity of appearance.' It's worthy of the approbation:
69 stones in a flattened oval, Meg herself (right) a 3.8-metre
sandstone megalith carved with cups, rings and grooves.

Common legend says that Meg was a 13th-century
witch called Meg Meldon and the ring was her nefarious
coven, all of whom were petrified by infamous Scottish
wizard (and one-time candidate for Archbishop of Canter-
bury) Michael Scott. Though other tales suggest that the
ring stones were her 69 lovers. No sniggering at the back!

Hunsonby, Penrith, Cumbria, CA10 1NW
Parking on site
///dried.reserve.richest

Long Meg (far right) and her Daughters – the third-widest stone circle in England.

Neolithic

Mayburgh

Tree-topped henge and a single megalith

Despite being spitting distance from the M6, few settings are as autumnal as this great, grassy banked henge – a perfect place to stop and scoff one's sandwiches on the way to or from the Scottish borders. It was built 4,500 years ago, the stones pulled from the nearby river and piled almost 6.5 metres tall in parts. There's an entrance portal to the east, facing the equinoctial dawn and, further on, another henge called King Arthur's Round Table. Its vertiginous banks are flecked with trees, and inside is a single megalith. Eighteenth-century antiquarian research reckons there would once have been seven megaliths present, but these were probably pilfered to build Eamont Bridge or Penrith Castle. Not that the ancients didn't exact revenge: lore tells that the thieves were tormented by their misdeed – one going mad and the other taking his own life.

Eamont Bridge, Cumbria, CA10 2BY
Parking 1KM away in Eamont Bridge village
///hypnotist.robot.sizing

Swinside Stone Circle

Picturesque ring, vandalised by Satan

Another Cumbrian circle of prestige, Swinside is unusual for its state of repair. Fifty-five of what were once 60 slate pillars – known locally as the 'grey cobbles' – remain (many now toppled), an incredibly high number in this world of tumbled rocks. This could be down to some canny architectural nous: surveys have shown that whoever constructed the circle engaged in some rudimentary landscaping, with the ground on which the stones stand levelled flat and a layer of foundation pebbles placed under the rocks.

Apocryphally, the stones are actually the topmost crenelations of a church, previously in a state of construction on the site, and which the Devil fiendishly pushed underground, creating the circle seen today (and hence the alternative name of 'Sunkenkirk', with 'kirk' a synonym for church). The story itself is a riff on the wider tradition of 'church sitting' tales, in which Lucifer, malevolent faeries or witches hoicked up holy foundations and moved them to other locations.

Swinside Fell, 8km north of Millom, Cumbria, LA18 5LD
Parking 2.5km away at the junction leading
to Swinside Farm, off the A595
///tonality.bulbs.bookcases

Neolithic and Bronze Age

Arbor Low and Gib Hill

Fantastic henge and nearby barrow

With only a 300-metre jaunt between them, mound fans get an effective two-for-one with the neighbouring sites of Arbor Low and Gib Hill. Arbor Low (right) is a resplendent, soul-stirring hump with 50 toppled limestone slabs and a 2-metre banked henge; the latter was once deemed 'the Stonehenge of the north' and a wonder of megalithic Britain by feted archaeologist Aubrey Burl. Gib Hill is a colossal, Neolithic oval barrow (with an ancillary Bronze Age round barrow tacked on at one end).

Arbor Low is undeniably the bigger hitter, not just for its central, tightly grouped stones (known as a cove) but for the dizzying scale of its construction. Almost 4,000 tonnes of limestone would have had to be hacked from the bedrock with antler picks to build the great bank. It's a riotous bargain, too – just a quid entry to the private farmland on which it sits.

Long Rake, Monyash, Bakewell, Derbyshire, DE45 1JS
Parking on site
///spoon.dumps.paint

Late Neolithic or early Bronze Age

Rudston Monolith

Pagan remnant on consecrated ground

The country's tallest standing stone – an absolute brute at 7.6 metres high, 2 metres wide, a metre thick and around 24 tonnes in weight – is in the churchyard of All Saints Rudston. It's a rather eerie (and almost irreverent) sight: the lofty menhir looming over the dead and their ornate Celtic crosses and headstones. A dinky lead cap was added to the stone in the 1700s to stem elemental erosion.

All Saints was built shortly after the Norman Conquest, but the site had likely been spiritually adulated for centuries before. The name Rudston may be a melding of the Old English 'rod' (cross) and 'stan' (stone), the inference being that a crosshead may have once been placed on the rock to override its Pagan origins. It's an iconic place out of time.

Rudston, Driffield, East Riding of Yorkshire, YO25 4UF
Parking in Rudston village
///lilac.enforced.speaks

Blakey Topping and Howden

Silbury inspiration in two sacred hills

Viewed from the southeast, the sacred hill of Blakey Topping (right) rises like a grand, comical pimple from the wild Yorkshire terrain. (It's rather flatter from the west, though equally deserving of archaeologist Jacquetta Hawkes' 'freakish-looking' verdict.) While meltwater erosion (literally, the flow of thawing glacier water shaping the land) is the likely cause, an ancillary legend states that it was created by a giant called Wade throwing a spadeful of earth at his wife, his crap aim creating the hill. Four standing stones sit sentinel at its base, which might once have been part of a larger circle.

Nearby, Howden Hill holds similarly soaring appeal, though rather more cosseted with sylvan greenery. This sacred clump is known to locals as both the Sugarloaf and, err, Tit Hill. Both, suggest various scholars, may well have been early inspiration for the creation of Wiltshire's finest conical hump, Silbury (p.54).

Blakey Topping, Pickering, North Yorkshire, YO18 7NR
Howden Hill, Langdale End, North Yorkshire, YO13 0BN
Roadside parking on site for both
///remains.clocking.solicitor ///beep.veered.pump

Bronze Age
Doll Tor, Derbyshire

This seminal woodland circle, looming low beneath creaking bows, is far more than the sum of its squat parts. Occasional excavations have thrown up urns, small cups and a host of burned human remains – a deathly ambience only fortifies the ageless scene.

Stanton Lees, Matlock, DE4 2LQ
///pursuit.falls.beaks

Bronze Age
Birkrigg Stone Circle, Cumbria

They've been battered over the years, so any historic alignments have been long rearranged, and the rocks are diminutive at best. However, these two circles offer charming views over the sodden flats of Morecambe Bay below.

Off the A5087, Ulverston, LA12 9RD
///fussed.grain.desktops

Neolithic
Twelve Apostles, West Yorkshire

A reconstructed circle off the Dales Way path, the enigmatic Apostles, also sometimes known by the less weirdly Christian name of the 'Druidical Dial', might be the most frequented ancient site in this part of the country – hence the disrepair (one smashed rock has been cemented back into shape).

Burley in Wharfedale, Ilkley, LS29 8BT
///feasts.billiard.eased

The Twelve Apostles stone circle, set on moorland
380 metres above sea level.

Bronze Age

The Devil's Arrows, North Yorkshire

Three stupendous stones found near the A1 motorway. The artsy grooving in the rock is natural, riven by thousands of years of trickling rainfall. Two other stones existed, but one was overturned by treasure hunters and then used to bridge a river, according to a 1577 edition of *Britannia*, while parts of the other are believed to have ended up as features in several local gardens.

Off the A1, Boroughbridge, YO51 9LW

///settled.premiums.wobbles

Bronze Age

Lordenshaw Main Rock, Northumberland

The gigantic slab of Lordenshaw Main Rock is decorated with the full palette of Bronze Age rock art. From rings and cups to grooves, channels and circles, this is a Celtic panoply of indeterminate purpose but misty intrigue.

Alnwick, Morpeth, NE65 7RP

///hires.shadows.edgy

Neolithic

Thornborough Henges, North Yorkshire

From the air, the immense rings of Thornborough look like a pair of crop circles. The appeal is headier at ground level; these monuments were also once dubbed 'the Stonehenge of the north'.

New Lane, West Tanfield, Ripon, DL8 2RD

///lawyer.overlook.loaded

*One of the Devil's Arrows – three Neolithic standing
stones near Boroughbridge, Yorkshire.*

Wales

Bryn Celli Ddu

Unrivalled wonder of a Welsh chamber mound

Opaquely translated as the 'Mound in the Dark Grove', this is one of the finest locales in a region brimming with ancient treasure. The huge chamber tomb is a spectacle. The steep-sided knoll rises dramatically from the surrounding circular henge ditch, its small entryway beckoning visitors into the antiquated gloom inside. It offers a few natty extra points of interest, too. There is a large rock outside the portal doorway, carved with a mysterious, faintly serpent-like (but ultimately unknowable) design. A concrete facsimile of the original, found buried in a pit, is now transposed to the National Museum of Wales. The chamber's entry passage is aligned to the Midsummer sunrise, which illuminates a polygonal central chamber with its own eerie blue-tinged pillar, the size of a man.

Near Llanddaniel Fab, Llanfair, Isle of Anglesey, LL61 6EQ
Parking on site
///vegetable.vibe.rates

The carved standing stone at the entrance to Bryn Celli Ddu.
Opposite: Bryn Celli Ddu's stone passageway.

Neolithic

Lligwy

Top-heavy, squat-legged tomb

A hulking tomb handily sat next to a road near Anglesey's east coast, Lligwy's USPs are twofold. First, its extremely squat dimensions: the capstone sits just a metre off the ground, though the standing rocks are half-buried, giving the impression of a massive petrified isopod (from some angles, anyway). Second, the absolutely enormous capstone itself: 5.9 metres long, 5.2 metres wide, a metre thick and weighing a cool 25 tonnes (the same as three T-Rexes, if you're after a truly arbitrary comparison). Raising the thing must have been an almost superhuman feat. The underlying space was a sombre home for around 30 bodies, as well as the usual scattershot selection of animal bones, flint tools, Neolithic grooved pottery and Bronze Age beakers.

Near Moelfre, Isle of Anglesey, LL72 8NH
Parking 2KM away in Moelfre village
///rumble.exotic.wreck

Bryn Cader Faner

A thorny crown in the middle of nowhere

Bryn Cader Faner ('The Hill with the Chair with the Flag' in Celtic) is an astounding Bronze Age round cairn. Nearly 9 metres across and replete with 18 jagged slate pillars, veined with quartz and jutting upwards at angles like a skeletal crown, it was likely constructed around 3000 BCE with a funerary function.

It's not the simplest to reach, requiring a 5-kilometre trudge across boggy terrain at a height of 380 metres. (Its 'Access' criteria receives a sullen 1 out of 5 on the excellent Megalithic Portal website.) But the intrepid can savour a fantastically barren and elemental scene – even despite the deconstructive efforts of antiquarian treasure hunters (whose hijinks can still be seen in the form of a central hole in the cairn) and the British Army, which used the mound for potshot gunnery practice during the Second World War.

Talsarnau, Gwynedd, LL47 6YU
Muddy 5KM walk from Eisingrug hamlet; parking in hamlet
///gaps.behalf.replayed

Gwâl y Filiast

Cute woodland cromlech with a hairy history

This is possibly the sweetest cromlech in Wales – the country's nomenclature for a dolmen tomb. Swooningly located on a misty, wooded ridge near the audibly roaring River Taff, this toadstool-like assemblage consists of four uprights and a stocky capstone. Cute until one deciphers the name, that is: Gwâl y Filiast means 'Lair of the Grey Hound Bitch', here a bastardisation of 'wolf' (rather than the sleek, speedy breed with a fancy for rabbits). It's also occasionally referred to as Dolwilym, or 'William's Meadow' in English (but there's scant evidence why, or who William was) and, more significantly, Arthur's Table. These tracts of Carmarthenshire were apocryphal hunting land for the mythical king, and the archaeologist Aubrey Burl even posited that the tomb was a kennel for his dog. Crucially, it's not to be confused with the identically named tomb in Glamorgan (p.166).

Whitland, Carmarthenshire, SA34 0TU
Parking 1KM away at the
Pen Y Bont Inn, Whitland, SA34 0XP
///shipwreck.depended.shoelaces

Neolithic

Gop Hill Cairn

North Wales' perfect sacred hump

Constructed between 4000 and 3000 BCE and soaring 244 metres into the air, this tapering knoll is the second-largest man-made mound in Britain and Ireland. It sits atop a hill known colloquially as 'The Gop' for its Welsh name of 'Gop-y-Goleuni', part of the Clwydian Range of mountains and only embellished by this knee-scraping cherry on top: one of Wales' biggest cairns, a mound of local limestone adding an extra 12 metres to the hill's already vertiginous dimensions. Below this sits a natural cave once used as a makeshift burial chamber for 14 souls. Its later history is almost as engaging: the hill sits above a grassy plane where the army of Queen Boudica is said to have been royally trounced by the Roman general Paulinus in 50 CE. It was also used as a 17th-century beacon, hence its alternative nickname, the 'Mound of Lights'.

Rhyl, Denbighshire, LL18 6DH
Parking 1KM away in Trelawnyd, LL18 6DT
///searcher.sprint.wins

Four Stones of Gwytherin

Four Pagan markers in a Christian churchyard

These four small uprights, aligned in a row from east to west, can be found in the circular yard of Gwytherin church. The yard's shape is an indicator that this Christian pile was constructed on what was likely Pagan ground – a fact compounded by the provision of ancient yew trees, a sacred symbol of early druidry. Their purpose and background is hazy as ever: a Latin inscription on one stone – 'Vinnemagli Fili / Senemagli', meaning 'of Vinnemaglus, son of Senemaglus' – is stylistically synonymous with the years 5 or 6 CE. Many believe the rocks to be a repurposed Bronze Age row, the site Christianised by missionaries spooked by their esoteric power.

1 Tai Newyddion, Gwytherin, Abergele, Conwy County Borough, LL22 8UT
Parking in Gwytherin village
///rivals.golf.topics

Neolithic

Tinkinswood

Magnificent barrow with a world-beating capstone

Wales has more than its share of stellar barrow tombs, but Tinkinswood threatens to take the prehistoric biscuit for the size of its capstone alone. Experts reckon that the huge boulder, weighing a cool 36 tonnes, would have needed around 200 brawny workers to lift it into place. 'A slightly cracked megalithic cereal bar of unfeasible antiquity,' wrote the questing antiquarian Julian Cope.

The entrance to the tomb is marked by a forecourt of intricate herringbone-patterned drywalling. Excavation revealed evidence of over 50 interred corpses of the Beaker folk – European emigrés who arrived in Britain 4,500 years ago – plus the bones of ox, sheep and pigs (perhaps the scraps from funeral feasts).

Great stuff, but heed caution: it's said that anyone who spends the night at Tinkinswood on the evenings before May Day, St John's Day (23 June) or the Winter Solstice will die, go mad or, *worse still*, become a poet.

Cardiff, CF5 6TA
Parking 0.2KM away on St. Nicholas to Dyffryn Gardens Road
///simulates.bared.succumbs

Neolithic

Arthur's Stone, Gower

Famously squat dolmen and possible timepiece

Sat on an achingly lovely stretch of the Gower Peninsula, the elevated boulder of Arthur's Stone (or 'Maen Ceti' in Welsh) is so laden with explanatory legend and academic intrigue that a speedy summation does scant justice. Some say the rock was a pebble found by King Arthur while on his way to battle, which was tossed here and swelled with pride from having met the king. Others claim that David, patron saint of Wales, struck the capstone with his sword, breaking off a piece as he railed against its Pagan origins. (The fragment now lies beside the main dolmen.) It was supposedly visited by Henry VIII's troops on the way to the Battle of Bosworth, was a huge tourist draw for the Victorians, and may even be a kind of rudimentary Celtic clock aligned with the movement of the stars.

Enigmas all, but its beatific setting and placement within a landscape strewn with cairns made it one of the first sites to be scheduled under the Ancient Monuments Act of 1882.

Northeast of Reynoldston, Swansea, SA3 1AE
Parking 0.5KM away at car park, SA3 1HA
///rehearsal.mourner.narrowest

Cwrt-y-Gollen Menhir

Lofty menhir on former MOD grounds

'MOD Property: No Trespassing, No Photography,' reads the haughty sign near this impressive menhir, jutting 4 metres from the earth outside an army cadet camp, once operated by the Ministry of Defence but long abandoned. Located just off the A40 between Crickhowell and Abergavenny, the River Usk a mere 300 metres away, the Sugar Loaf mountain rising to the east and – at the time of writing – a hot-pink burger van parked just across the road, the incongruous setting only adds to the allure of this red sandstone pillar. Local tradition infers that the rock is impossible to accurately measure and that it is constantly swelling in size, hence the alternative name of 'The Growing Stone'. But even at its extant scale, it's a vision, 'straining at the earth and your perceptions of normality', as RiotGibbon, a user on the online forum Modern Antiquarian, writes rather poetically.

Cwrt-y-gollen, Crickhowell, Powys, NP8 1EE
Parking on site
///market.waggled.strength

Neolithic

Trefignath

Striking portal tomb on industrial edgelands

It's somewhat lacking the bucolic solitude of many sacred places, sure – but Trefignath's proximity to the A55 and an aluminium reduction plant does at least afford it some gritty edge. The chamber itself is a rather weathered and tumbled construction with a duo of two-metre portal stones that would have once granted entry to a long, multi-chambered tomb built over centuries. Later restorations were a bit slap-dash but 20th-century archaeology doyenne Jacquetta Hawkes still deemed Trefignath 'an idea of megalithic archi-tecture at its grandest'. Intriguingly, she also suggested that the style was redolent of similar tombs in Ulster and south-west Scotland, hinting at an abundance of nautical traffic around the Irish Sea in this bygone era.

Near Trearddur, south of Holyhead, Holy Island,
Isle of Anglesey, LL65 2YW
Parking and train station 2.5KM away in Holyhead
///shows.presented.joggers

Pentre Ifan

Fantastically positioned and painterly dolmen

Behold the most immediately recognisable monument in Wales' prehistoric pantheon. Pentre Ifan elevates the ubiquitous chamber into something palpably dreamlike. Its hefty, 16-tonne capstone, suspended on the pin-sharp points of three uprights, gives the impression of almost hovering above them. Three further stones form a skeletal portal; another stands in the doorway.

The scene was made even more phantasmagoric by the painter Richard Tongue – an ardent documentarian of prehistoric monuments – in 1835. His painting stretches and slightly twists the pillars into something more abstractly humanoid, transforms the gently undulating hills into precipitous scarps and adds a doleful shepherd to complete the scene. Tongue leaves out the faeries who are said to frequent the site in local folklore (inexplicably clad in red caps and soldiers' uniform, according to the tales).

Nevern, Crymych, Pembrokeshire, SA41 3TZ
Parking on site
///mingles.cups.premiums

Neolithic

Carreg Samson

Giant dolmen with a lustrous streak

A thwacking great 5,000-year-old Neolithic cromlech located half a mile west of Abercastle Bay near the Pembrokeshire Coast Path, Carreg Samson's improbable scale is only bolstered by its lovely aspect of the Irish Sea's shining levels. It's named for the Welsh Saint Samson, who was said to have placed the heaving capstone, perched like a gargantuan hat on seven triangular uprights, with a single finger (a fine yarn, undermined by the fact that Samson wasn't born until the relatively modern 5th century CE).

Also known as the 'Longhouse', the dolmen may have been part of a chamber tomb or a passage, and certainly a sheep shelter a century ago. A glimpse under the capstone reveals a luminous bonus: a gleaming vein of amber quartzite, enlivening the stone's muted hues.

Haverfordwest, Pembrokeshire, SA62 5HJ
Parking 0.8KM away (via Pembrokeshire Coast Path) at
Abercastle harbour, SA62 5HJ
///crumble.able.shuttling

Wales

Carreg Samson's robust cromlech peers over the Irish Sea.

Neolithic
Coetan Arthur, Pembrokeshire

Hiding among the myriad boulders strewn on a hillside next to St. David's Head – a joyful wildflower heaven of a Pembrokeshire headland laden with ancient bits and pieces – Coetan Arthur is a collapsed, low-slung dolmen. Its butt rests on the ground and its opposing end is propped up on an orthostat (a slab of a rock placed artificially upright, as part of a wider ancient structure).

St. David's, Haverfordwest, SA62 6PS
///practical.storms.stockpile

Bronze Age
Penrhos Feilw, Isle of Anglesey

This looming duo of spiky, spindly menhirs sits on a grassy plain between two diminutive hills. Their history – the whys, whats and whens – is reliably murky, maintaining a spectral character despite the proximity to Holy Island's mundane modern life. There are spanking views of the bay at Trearddur, too.

Penrhos Feilw, Holyhead, Holy Island, LL65 2LU
///assess.essay.outcasts

Neolithic
Dolmen Bachwen, Gwynedd

A cracking cromlech tomb in the distant shadow of Gyrn Goch, waxing from the ground like a giant skate ramp. A snoop atop the Bachwen's capstone reveals an extra level of textural nuance: more than 100 cup marks carved over its weathered expanse, the purpose of which remains per-plexingly vague.

Clynnog-fawr, Caernarfon, LL54 5NN
///routine.spoils.feasting

Neolithic
Pont-y-Pridd Rocking Stone, Rhondda Cynon Taf

These wonderful prehistoric stacked stones near Ponty-pridd hospital are supplemented by a modern circle. The latter was installed by the Gorsedd (a semi-druidic group of Welsh-speaking writers, musicians and artists) for an Eisteddfod festival of Welsh heritage in 1849. Ersatz it may be, but the heady aura is undeniable.

Common Road, Pontypridd, CF37 4AH
///cure.tender.unfair

Bronze Age
Maen Llia, Powys

Sat in a blissfully solitary position in the rolling Brecon Beacons (and easily visited via a small road near the village of Ystradfellte), the name of this hoofing, 3.7-metre nugget of a stone translates as 'The Stone That Licks'. It's a riff on how, on Midsummer's Eve, the shadow cast by the sunset stretches down the hill and over a stream, from which the stone is said to drink. *Iechyd da!* (That's 'cheers!' in Welsh.)

Sarn Helen, Brecon, LD3 8SU
///compress.maple.display

Bronze Age

Moel Ty-Uchaf, Denbighshire

This 41-stone circle is dinky in stature (each being a mere 60 centimetres or less) but huge in subtext. It was once described by architectural professor and sacred geometer Keith Critchlow as 'perhaps the most geometrically sophisticated of all the Neolithic structures', channelling the idea that certain stone circles reflected astrological alignments. This might also explain a supposed UFO sighting above the hill in 1974. Cosmic stuff.

Llandrillo, Corwen, LL20 7LH
///exclusive.tilting.disarmed

Neolithic

St. Lythans, Vale of Glamorgan

A near neighbour of Tinkinswood (p.150) to the north, the imposing tomb of St. Lythans also goes by the name of Gwâl y Filiast (like the one in Carmarthenshire on p.144), though this time because of its supposed use as a dog shelter in the 1800s (unlike the former, which was an apocryphal kennel for King Arthur's pooch). Far sweeter is an attached tale that, each Midsummer's Eve, the moss-flecked capstone spins around and the rest of the rocks take themselves to the nearby river Waycock for a dip.

Wenvoe, CF5 6SU
///inspects.computers.boats

Moel Ty-Uchaf stone circle, the site of
a (still unexplained) UFO sighting in 1974.

Scotland

Machrie Moor Standing Stones

A bevy of rings in a rich prehistoric landscape

A fecund hub of antiquarian delights, Arran's Machrie Moor is dotted with stone rings, lonely megaliths, cist graves, burial cairns and early field systems. They're all wonders, but its six stone circles are especially striking. They were first recorded in 1861, each simply named 'Machrie Moor' and numbered 1–5. The sixth emerged from the peat in 1978 and was subsequently dubbed Machrie Moor 11 (numbers 6–10 correspond to the other glut of ancient sites discovered prior).

Machrie Moor 2 (right) is the complex's undeniable looker, comprising three vertiginous, otherworldly spindles. Machrie Moor 5 boasts two rings of squat granite boulders, also known as 'Fingal's Cauldron Seat' – the hole in one of the stones said to be where the giant Fingal (protagonist of a series of 18th-century epic poems) tied up his dog. Some also claim it's the home of a faerie, who can be placated by pouring milk into the recess.

Off the western coastal road, Isle of Arran, KA27 8DX
Parking on site
///dates.assurance.tastes

Aikey Brae Stone Circle

Perfect circle with a first-rate recumbent

Aberdeenshire could well be considered the spiritual home of the recumbent stone circle – simply, a ring that includes a single giant megalith reclining on its side rather than upright. The region is home to around 70 of these horizontal heroes, but few are as hauntingly evocative as Aikey Brae: a 16-metre ringed bank enclosing five erect rocks and a leviathan, 21.5-tonne prone stone, lying down as a visual centrepiece. The circle once sat beside an evergreen woodland, sadly felled in 2019, but the spot remains woozily atmospheric, peering over the surrounding countryside and ruin of Deer Abbey, a 13th-century monastery.

Naturally, Aikey Brae's purpose remains vague, but experts have guessed that the site layout held some kind of cosmic significance. Even more vividly, a 2001 excavation discovered that the kerbstones in the circle's ring bank alternated in colour between red and white. Information on why this may be is similarly scant, but they make a fine technicolour perk to an already unparalleled place.

Old Deer, Peterhead, Aberdeenshire, AB42 5PP
Parking on farm track off the A950 and B9029 roads,
where the circle is signposted
///beginning.ramps.giant

Scotland

Clava Cairns

Three trend-setting mounds near the Nairn

Positioned in a line and situated stumbling distance from the site of the Battle of Culloden (where the British smashed the poor Jacobite rebels in 1746), these three monumental pebble-piles gave their name to the 50 or so similar mounds dotted around the Inverness area. ('Clava-style' refers to ring-shaped grave chambers of two variations: the first topped with a roof of heaped stones and entered via a passage; the second entirely open to the sky.)

The northeastern pile is the most resplendent: 3 metres high, now without its covering structure but surrounded by a weathered circle. Some archaeologists reckoned that paths of rubble would have extended from the centre, making the whole thing look rather like an oversized bicycle wheel. The central cairn (pictured at the top here) is a sealed ring of stones with no entrance and a chamber open to the elements. The third (pictured below) is identical to the first. As with many other tombs of this kind, the position of the sun's rays on the Winter Solstice would have purposefully illuminated the then-covered passages.

Southeast of Leanach, near Culloden, Highland, IV2 5EJ
Parking on site
///abstracts.stirs.funny

Cairnholy 1 and 2

Two startlingly spiky tombs

Here is a double hit of cairn chamber action with dreamy aspects across Wigtown Bay's gleaming wash. The tombs are constructed in the Clyde style, typical to around 100 old-world settings in this part of Scotland: a grave without a passageway, entry instead provided via a forecourt without a roof, usually fronted by colossal stones.

Cairnholy 1 is the more arresting of the two, its eight jagged forecourt shards straining into the sky. The name is a possible bastardisation of Carn Ulaidh, or the 'Treasure Cairn'. Indeed, a 1941 excavation threw up a delicate jadeite axe head – a natty Neolithic object of prestige, given the verdant mineral was originally mined far away in the Italian Alps and brought to Scotland via ancient trade routes.

Cairnholy 2 (right), 150 metres away, is a more diminutive treat: a low-slung chamber with a rectangular capstone and another great finger of an entrance pillar, traditionally thought to be the grave of the mythical king Caldus.

Off the A75, east of Creetown, Newton Stewart,
Dumfries and Galloway, DG8 7EA
Parking on site
///hiker.talents.register

Achnabreck Cup and Ring Marks

Swirl-covered slab of epic proportions

Achnabreck – meaning 'Rock of the Host' in Gaelic – represents the apex of prehistoric rock art in Scotland. This giant stone slab, buried in the landscape of Kilmartin Glen (a piping hotbed of primitive titillation), is covered in carved rings, spirals, ringed stars and parallel lines. The myriad designs overlay each other – implying they were created over a long period – and are most dramatically visible during bad weather, when the rain flows through and accentuates the grooves.

Intriguingly, the meanings of these designs may have depended on their elevation. More complex motifs, such as those found on Achnabreck, are ubiquitous to lowland areas; more restrained ones are found decorating higher-up sites. Either way, Achnabreck is a debossed icon and, if we're being grandiose, an alfresco doodle to rival Europe's finest cave paintings.

Near Cairnbaan, northwest of Lochgilphead,
Argyll and Bute, PA31 8SG
Parking 5KM away in Lochgilphead, PA31 8NN
///curving.reflector.look

Scotland

Standing Stones
of Lundin

Three above-par uprights on a golfing green

This genuinely oddball-looking trio of stones is quite unlike anything else in this book, not least for being plonked ignominiously in the middle of a fairway at the estimable Lundin Links golf course. They're certainly surreal. There is something almost Dalí-esque about the natural, curvaceous sandstone fluting and their elongated, quirky positioning against the massive sky behind. (Twentieth-century archaeologist Aubrey Burl described them as 'writhing', which is also pretty accurate.) The towering group – up to 5.2 metres in height – was once a megalithic quartet, but one stone is long-lost, tipped over by treasure hunters aeons ago.

The surrounding hills also thrum with antique energy; sheep on the nearby ancient volcano Largo Law were once said to return from grazing with golden fleeces, supposedly due to a provision of hidden treasure buried under the hill.

At Lundin Golf Club, 9 Golf Road, Fife, KY8 6AJ
Parking in Lundin Links village
///wove.added.pages

Neolithic

Croft Moraig

Multi-era marvel on a gentle raise

Located a mere 50-metre stroll from the road – but overshadowed by both a farmhouse and some corrugated agricultural buildings – the dwarfish, blink-and-you'll-miss-it vibe of this fantastic amalgam of ages belies its abiding power.

Its construction was protracted, commencing with a horseshoe of wooden posts erected around 3000 BCE, later replaced with rocks. At some point, a rubble bank and an eight-stone circle hemming the horseshoe in were added. Later still, an additional three stones were dragged to the site, including a cup-marked horizontal stone, believed to be a marker of the southern moonset. And finally, another nine stones were set in place to enclose the first circle.

The setting may not always have been so modest. There was once a nearby hamlet called Styx, a name that may have been a reworking of the Gaelic 'stuicnean' (a ground of overturned trees), implying that the circles may once have been more arcanely set in dense oak wood.

South side of the A827 by Croftmoraig Farm,
west of Aberfeldy, Perth and Kinross, PH15 2EY
Parking on site
///orbited.uniform.parent

Lochbuie Standing Stones

Dank approach and a petal-lined prize

Auspicious for being Mull's only stone circle, Lochbuie comprises eight heaving hunks of granite (a long-lost ninth is marked with a boulder). Twelve metres in diameter, the circle is sat in the grounds of the eponymous house, belonging to the local Clan MacLaine of Lochbuie. The setting – in the shadow of the resplendently rugged, mist-shrouded Ben Buie and closely ringed by hot pink rhododendron – is dreamlike. The approach, however, is more of a trial. A series of painted-white rocks (plus a smattering of planks and makeshift bridges) lead the seeker through a boggy pasture, past an outlying guard-stone two metres in height (vaguely aligned with the position of Midwinter's Solstice sunset) and a chestnut-tree-ringed cairn, to the triangular and lichen-flecked circle itself. It's an uncommon sight in the western reaches of Scotland, rings of rocks clearly not being in fashion round these parts. Wellies essential, whatever time of year.

Lochbuie House, Lochbuie, Isle of Mull, PA62 6AA
Parking 1.4KM away at Laggan Beach
///camp.engraving.will

Stanydale

A mysterious 'temple' in the north island wilds

Tribal community centre? Chieftain's home? Elaborate tomb? The purpose of the huge, heel-shaped recess of Stanydale, set among mainland Shetland's primitive field systems and Neolithic houses, remains opaque. When the site was first excavated in 1949, it was even believed to be a holy place in thrall to the incredible Neolithic shrines of distant Malta, such were the weird similarities in design. This is now seen as rather far-fetched, even if the 'temple' tag and assumed ritual use has prevailed.

In any case, it's quite unlike anything else in Scotland. Chunky, 3.7-metre-thick walls encircle an expansive room, while a duo of post holes suggest that the structure may have been roofed at some point in its history. Interestingly, excavations have failed to turn up the usual prehistoric domestic detritus (bits of bone, shards of pottery and so on), the meticulous neatness suggesting a place of some estimable status. Tidy.

Near Bixter, The Mainland, Shetland, ZE2 9NS
Parking 1.6KM away off the A971
///impresses.slimming.analogy

Shetland's Stanydale, initially labelled as a temple for its striking design similarities with Neolithic shrines in Malta.

The Heart of Neolithic Orkney

Spectacular group of timeworn titans

The Heart of Neolithic Orkney is a congregation of ancient locales barely believable in prestige and scale, all located on the archipelago's largest island, Mainland.

First, Maeshowe: Scotland's superlative chambered cairn, 8 kilometres east of Stromness town. The mound was excavated in 1861, revealing a host of 12th-century graffiti scrawled by Norsemen. One especially thrilling (if unfounded) note read: 'It is long ago that a great treasure was hidden here.' What's more, the *Orkneyinga saga* – a medieval chronicle and narrative history of the islands – includes an eerie tale of Vikings who sheltered overnight in the tomb, going violently insane as a result. Be wary. A tight opening crawl passage belies a network of tunnels, rooms and a vaulting central chamber, which (surprise!) is illuminated by the sunset at the Winter Solstice. Zero human remains have been found at Maeshowe, leading some to compare the site to the Great Pyramid of Giza: a cosmic observatory rather than a tomb.

A short stumble along a Neolithic road reveals the stones of Stenness – four magnificent, towering shards up to 5 metres in height. Like Maeshow, Stenness was a locale for Norse ritual – to such an extent that, on Christmas ▶

Skara Brae, Europe's most complete example of a Neolithic village.

The Stones of Stenness, towering stones of up to 5 metres in height.

Day 1814, one tenant farmer decided to topple the stones to discourage spiritualist tourists tramping his adjacent land. A suspension order was passed, but only after he'd smashed the beloved 'Odin Stone' – one of Scotland's most mythologically charged sites, visited by lovers who'd make their vows through a notched hole in the rock.

Next looms the Ring of Brodgar, a phenomenal stone circle, its one-time collection of 60 rocks now reduced to just 29. Look out for the scratchy Norse designs that festoon some of the stones (an anvil and, sweetly, the name 'Bjorn' among them).

Finally, schlep north to the Bay of Skaill and Skara Brae. Europe's most complete example of a Neolithic village system was revealed to the world in 1840 when a violent storm upended a dune and uncovered eight prehistoric dwellings. The intrigue lies in the hordes of stone-carved domestic equipment found within – from box beds and water tanks, to hearths, cupboards, dressers, a basic sewer system and even a jolly skull-drilling trepanning tool.

It's worth noting that these places are largely older than Stonehenge by a millennium – a radiant topography of incredible antique importance.

Parking on site for all monuments
Maeshowe: ///central.helper.recording
Ring of Brodgar: ///patrol.rezoning.older
Stones of Stenness: ///liberated.dusty.scribbled
Skara Brae: ///epidemics.trails.tingled

*Maeshowe, Orkney's chambered cairn, fancifully thought to be
a kind of cosmic observatory rather than a tomb.
Opposite: The Ring of Brodgar stone circle.*

Calanais Stones

Sprawling stone cross in a sleepy landscape

This cross-shaped collection of 40 or so rocks with a single pillar at its nexus may be the most beloved stones in the Hebrides. Fashioned in Lewisian gneiss – a faintly marbled metamorphic rock, and one of the oldest materials in the country – they sit at the head of northwest Lewis' Loch Roag.

The site is thought to have been laid out according to the southern lunar standstill (when the northernmost and southernmost moonrise and moonset appear furthest apart). Here, the moon at this mystically loaded juncture rises above the thighs of the Sleeping Beauty – a series of distant hills that make the shape of a dozing woman – before zipping across the cross's eastern expanse of stones, dipping behind a rocky outcrop and swiftly reappearing in its full, shimmering majesty in the centre of the circle. Nearly as entrancing is the tale of a shining figure who walks the central stone avenue at Midsummer, accompanied by a cuckoo – the bird of Tír na nÓg, the Celtic land of the gods.

Off the A858, west of Stornoway, Isle of Lewis, HS2 9DY
Parking on site
///bluff.holds.deprive

Scotland

Bronze Age
Nether Largie Standing Stones, Argyll and Bute

Bedfellows to Achnabreck's swirling carvings (p.178) in the ancient hotbed of Kilmartin Glen, Nether Largie's five stones top out at a vertiginous 3 metres in height – the largest of which is covered in dimple-like cup and ring marks. Camping near them is said to bring good luck, though actually touching them supposedly brings terrible misfortune. Hands off!

Baluachraig, PA31 8QF
///tinkle.micro.nametag

Bronze Age
Tyrebagger, Aberdeenshire

In the Aberdeen hinterland of Dyce, this recumbent stone circle is (conveniently) set above a farm called Standing-stones. Tyrebagger was once appropriated as a cattle pound, the interior space hollowed out and the space between the stones filled to create a rustic pen. The cows long shooed away, the ring is now returned to its former glory, peeking from a copse in juxtaposition with nearby Aberdeen International Airport.

Aberdeen, AB21 0HH
///canoe.extension.pose

Ballochmyle Cup and Ring Marks, East Ayrshire

Found in 1986 – when a work party on a nearby estate cleared foliage away from a rock face on the grounds – Ballochmyle's hugely extensive rock art features cup and ring marks, stars within circles, squares, rectangles and other abstract shapes thought to be deer. Celestial charts? Way-markings? Pictorial appeasements of the gods? As ever, it's all rather foggy.

Mauchline, KA5 5JX
///bikers.chaos.shampoos

Neolithic

Aquhorthies Stone Circle, Aberdeenshire

This is a banger of a ring cairn, beautifully preserved and in its original formation (no lazy re-erections here). Eight granite and one red jasper stone sit in a slightly squished circle – though the invariable focus is a handsome, red-granite horizontal rock, positioned like a Pagan altar, with two smaller flank stones on either side. The devotional atmosphere is echoed in the name – Aquhorthies translates as 'Field of Prayer' in Scots Gaelic.

Stonehaven, AB39 3PD
///charities.cable.pleasing

Bronze Age

Kintraw, Argyll and Bute

Midwinter intrigue abounds with this striking, spectacularly positioned 4-metre pillar looming over Loch Craignish. The cairn closest to it is thought to have once been covered in gleaming white quartz, the duo aligned to the setting solstice sun through a notch in the distant Paps of Jura mountains. A neat additional legend says that it was erected over the grave of a Norse prince, hence its occasional name, 'The Danish King's Grave'.

Lochgilphead, PA31 8UW
///sour.alleyway.stags

Kintraw standing stone, at the head of Loch Craignish.

The Experts

Many archaeologists, antiquarians and historians have given their two cents on the monuments in this book. Below are some of the most significant – and colourful – figures.

William Stukeley

In the pantheon of elaborately coiffed and fusty religious antiquarians, none come bigger than Bill Stukely. Working in the early to mid 1700s, the man was a major figure in the scholarly exploration of totemic hotspots like Avebury and Stonehenge.

Rev. William Borlase

An 18th-century Cornish antiquarian, naturalist and rector. Rev. Borlase is best remembered for books like the 1754 touchstone *The Antiquities of Cornwall* and was an enthusiastic recorder of his home county's ancient sites. This, though – says Oxford's Ashmolean Museum – was predominantly down to being hamstrung by a lack of spare cash that would've allowed him to gallivant further afield to the prehistoric locales of Europe. Cost of living, eh?

Jacquetta Hawkes

Joyfully insolent, wildly readable and hyper-chic 20th-century archaeologist and author, and a titan in prehistoric history. Her 1951 book *A Land* is a stone-cold (arf!) classic, and she was archaeological advisor to the Festival of Britain the same year.

James Dyer

Author of Faber & Faber's 1973 prosaically titled and indispensable *Southern England: An Archaeological Guide*. The text is charmingly curmudgeonly at times, but the research (and the retro cover design) is absolutely second to none. Glyn Daniel – the man who defined the Cotswold-Severn style of chamber tombs – was also its editor. Catnip for barrow fiends, in other words.

Aubrey Burl

Dubbed 'the enthusiast's megalithic expert' by the *Guardian*, Burl was the 20th to early 21st century's key archaeological mind on all things stones (indeed, he published a whacking 19 books on British stone circles alone). In this book, he occasionally crops up as a definitive voice on the subject; the man who bridged the gap between the fusty historians of old and today's hipster cache on matters of antiquity.

Julian Cope

Leather-clad post-punk figurehead (and main man in Liverpool's The Teardrop Explodes), Cope later became the definitive neo-antiquarian via classic books *The Modern Antiquarian* and *The Megalithic European* – incredible, gonzo tomes suffused with a kind of misty-eyed and otherworldly reverence for the places written about that sets him apart from almost every other budding stone-devotee out there. Essential stuff.

Megalithic Media

This book is merely one of many gateways to the sites of ancient Britain. The shortlist of publications and websites below are all invaluable resources and romping good reads in their own rights. We've also curated a selection of stones on-screen – some straight, some hokey – along with records that either have a direct connection to the topic (Aphex Twin's quiet fascination with the bygone landscapes of his native Cornwall; Mulholland literally recording the close groans of rocks) or simply provided the appropriate vibe while researching this book.

Books

Bill Anderton, *Guide to Ancient Britain* (1991)

Geoffrey Ashe, *Mythology Of The British Isles* (2002)

Janet and Colin Bord, *A Guide to Ancient Sites in Britain* (1978)

Andy Burnham (ed), *The Old Stones: A Field Guide to the Megalithic Sites of Britain and Ireland* (2018)

Aubrey Burl, *The Stone Circles of the British Isles* (1977)

Rodney Castleden, *Ancient British Hill Figures* (1999)

Ithell Colquhoun, *The Living Stones: Cornwall* (1957)

Julian Cope, *The Modern Antiquarian* (1998)

James Dyer, *Southern England: An Archaeological Guide* (1973)

Dave Hamilton, *Wild Ruins BC* (2019)

Jacquetta Hawkes, *A Guide to the Prehistoric and Roman Monuments in England and Wales* (1973)

Colin Richards and Vicki Cummings, *Stone Circles: A Field Guide* (2024)

Adam Thorpe, *On Silbury Hill* (2014)

Jennifer Westwood and Jacqueline Simpson, *Lore of The Land: A Guide To England's Myths And Legends* (2005)

Ordnance Survey, *Ancient Britain* (2016)

Weird Walk, *Weird Walk: Wanderings and Wonderings Through the British Ritual Year* (2023)

Websites

Atlas Obscura: atlasobscura.com

English Heritage: english-heritage.org.uk

Historic Environment Scotland: portal.historicenvironment.scot

The Megalithic Portal: megalithic.co.uk

The Modern Antiquarian: themodernantiquarian.com

National Trust: nationaltrust.org.uk

Northern Antiquarian: thenorthernantiquarian.org

Stone Circles: stone-circles.org.uk

Stone Club: stoneclub.rocks

Film / Television

Darrol Blake (dir), *Doctor Who: The Stones of Blood* (1978)

Jeremy Deller, *Everybody in the Place: an Incomplete History of Britain* (1984–1992, 2019)

Lawrence Gordon Clark (dir), *Stigma* (1977)

Peter Graham Scott (dir), *Children of the Stones* (1977)

Sid Hope and Freddie Miller, *Free the Stones!* (2025)

Derek Jarman, *A Journey to Avebury* (1977)

Rob Reiner (dir), *This is Spinal Tap* (1984)

Paul Wright (dir), *Arcadia* (2017)

Music

Alison Cotton, *All Is Quiet At The Ancient Theatre* (2018)

Aphex Twin, *Richard D. James Album* (1996)

Belbury Poly, *Farmer's Angle* (2004)

James Holden, *The Inheritors* (2013)

Drew Mulholland, *The Making Of Landscape* (2016)

Richard Skelton, *Landings* (2010)

XTC, *English Settlement* (1982)

Many thanks to Ally, Andrew, Ruby, Rosie, Phoebe, Erin, Paulo, Philip, Rob, Adam, Dulcie, Jodie and Basil for their patience and (I believe) sincere interest in the rambling (literally and figuratively) that took form in this book. Thanks, too, to Flo, Dom, Martin and Ann at Hoxton Mini Press for taking a punt and bringing the old stones to life in such reliably pithy style.

Tom Howells

Tom Howells is a journalist and editor, who has written for the *Financial Times*, *Vogue*, *The Quietus*, *FACT*, *The Fence*, *World of Interiors*, *Wallpaper**, *London Design Festival* and more. He's happiest when drifting the Neolithic barrows and stones of the Isle of Wight and once got locked in Carisbrooke Castle.

Hoxton Mini Press

Hoxton Mini Press is a small independent publisher based in east London. We are committed to making beautiful but affordable books that don't screw up the planet. We offset all our printing, and we hope that the trees we do use will continue their life as beautiful books that you'll pass on to your grandchildren.

Ancient Britain for Modern Folk
First edition

Published in 2025 by Hoxton
Mini Press, London
Copyright © Hoxton Mini Press
2025. All rights reserved.

Text by Tom Howells
Editing by Florence Ward
Design & production by Dom Grant
Proofreading by Madeleine Pollard
Editorial support by Richard Enright

The right of Tom Howells to
be identified as the creator of
this Work has been asserted
under the Copyright, Designs
and Patents Act 1988.

Thank you to all of the individuals
and institutions who have provided
images and arranged permissions.
While every effort has been made to
trace the present copyright holders
we apologise in advance for any
unintentional omission or error,
and would be pleased to insert the
appropriate acknowledgement in any
subsequent edition.

A CIP catalogue record for this book
is available from the British Library.

ISBN: 978-1-914314-91-9

Printed and bound by
OZGraf, Poland

Manufacturer: Hoxton Mini Press,
104 Northside Studios,
16-29 Andrews Road,
London, E8 4QF
www.hoxtonminipress.com

Represented by: Authorised Rep
Compliance Ltd., Ground Floor,
71 Lower Baggot Street,
Dublin, D02 P593, Ireland
www.arccompliance.com

Hoxton Mini Press is an
environmentally conscious publisher,
committed to offsetting our carbon
footprint. This book is 100 per cent
carbon compensated, with offset
purchased from Stand For Trees.

Every time you order from our
website, we plant a tree:
www.hoxtonminipress.com

MIX
Paper | Supporting
responsible forestry
FSC® C163799
FSC
www.fsc.org